Math Memories You Can Count On

A Literature-based Approach to Teaching Mathematics in the Primary Classrooms

Jo-Anne Lake

Pembroke Publishers Limited

To my beloved grandchildren, Benjamin, Noah, and Avery.
May you learn the powerful connection of math to everyday life
and real-world situations.

© 2009 Pembroke Publishers
538 Hood Road
Markham, Ontario, Canada L3R 3K9
www.pembrokepublishers.com

Distributed in the U.S. by Stenhouse Publishers
480 Congress Street
Portland, ME 04101
www.stenhouse.com

We acknowledge the financial support of the Government of Canada through the Book Publishing Industry Development Program (BPIDP) for our publishing activities.

We acknowledge the assistance of the Government of Ontario through the Ontario Media Development Corporation's Ontario Book Initiative.

Library and Archives Canada Cataloguing in Publication

Lake, Jo-Anne
    Math memories you can count on : a literature-based approach to teaching mathematics in the primary classrooms / Jo-Anne Lake.

Includes index.
ISBN 978-1-55138-227-2

    1. Mathematics—Study and teaching (Primary). 2. Mathematics and literature—Study and teaching (Primary). I. Title.

QA135.6.L35 2008   372.7'044   C2008-903751-0

Editor: Alan Simpson, Kat Mototsune
Cover Design: John Zehethofer
Typesetting: Jay Tee Graphics Ltd.

Printed and bound in Canada
9 8 7 6 5 4 3 2 1

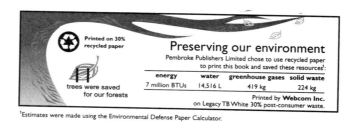

Printed on 30% recycled paper

trees were saved for our forests

Preserving our environment
Pembroke Publishers Limited chose to use recycled paper to print this book and saved these resources[1]:

energy	water	greenhouse gases	solid waste
7 million BTUs	14,516 L	419 kg	224 kg

Printed by **Webcom Inc.** on Legacy TB White 30% post-consumer waste.

[1]Estimates were made using the Environmental Defense Paper Calculator.

FSC
Mixed Sources
Product group from well-managed forests, controlled sources and recycled wood or fiber
Cert no. SW-COC-002358
www.fsc.org
© 1996 Forest Stewardship Council

Contents

Preface

Using children's literature as a strategy to teach mathematics in primary classrooms can create long-lasting positive math memories. A substantial base of mathematical understanding is set in the first few years of schooling. *(Early Math Strategy Report,* 1999.) Ongoing research suggests that "literature provides a contextual base by embedding the meaning of the math in situations to which children can relate." (*NCTM News Bulletin,* 2000.) In their field experiences, prospective teachers have underscored the importance of linking the literature with real-life connections to build positive math memories for all students.

There is a variety of children's literature for this literature-based approach to teaching math in the primary classroom. With planning and thoughtful selection, teachers can use literature to:

- create memorable math memories
- link math skills and concepts embedded in the context of story
- help children see how math will be useful to them in the "real world"

Appealing children's books such as Bruce Goldstone's *Great Estimations* and Stuart J. Murphy's *Betcha!—Estimating* are two excellent ways to begin you and your students' journey into the exciting concept of connecting children's literature and real-world applications.

This quote from a future teacher illustrates the value of using children's literature to instill a meaningful understanding of math concepts and their real-world applications:

I was able to experience firsthand how using children's literature to help students understand the concept of estimation can lead to real-life applications for students.

Here, the prospective teacher further reflects on how using children's literature helped his students begin to develop both an understanding of the concept of estimation and real-world connections that lead to positive math memories:

I learned that linking to real-life examples in a math lesson can increase students' interest and enthusiasm. During my practicum, the students used the background they acquired from working with the appropriate literature selections to estimate and calculate the speed of cars travelling on the street in front of their school. Police officers were invited to use radar guns to confirm the speed of the cars. This math activity culminated in the story being broadcast on the local news channel.

I have spent thirty years teaching Kindergarten to Grade 8; I devoted a lot of effort in the last ten years to tracking down and exploring children's books that can provide strong links to mathematics for primary-classrooms teachers. Over the years, I have worked with and listened to pre-service and experienced teachers speak of their math memories. These math memories were the catalyst that sparked my renewed interest in providing new insight into the effective teaching of mathematics—sharing relevant and memorable math stories for students. Children's literature is a powerful vehicle for teaching mathematics in primary classrooms. I have searched out the best children's books in the form of story, rhyme, song, and other literary styles to help teachers build positive math attitudes for all children in the primary grades. It's my belief that children deserve to leave school confident in their ability to know, understand, and do math.

Math Memories You Can Count On is a literature-based approach to teaching math in the primary grades. This guide assists teachers in selecting, organizing, and using children's literature as an effective strategy for teaching mathematics. Children's fiction and non-fiction books help students learn key mathematical concepts and processes: problem solving, reasoning and proof, communication, making connections, and representing math in a variety of ways. Collectively, the development of these processes plays a fundamental role in developing students' conceptual understanding of math. Throughout this book, prospective and experienced teachers share "real" math memories and math reflections. These meaningful math memories reinforce the book's underpinning message: Positive Math Memories + Positive Math Attitudes = Higher Levels of Achievement in Mathematics that last throughout a lifetime.

Math Memories You Can Count On explores math-literature connections in a variety of literary genres and offers suggestions for extending and applying them in the primary classroom. There is no shortage of children's literature for the primary classroom. With planning and thoughtful selection, teachers can use literature to:

- enhance students' natural interest in mathematics
- encourage students to explain their thinking as they interact with math
- strengthen problem-solving and reasoning abilities

Math Memories You Can Count On goes beyond "reading" about math by offering appropriate hands-on activities that bring all aspects of math to life and help students gain firsthand experience with appropriate math manipulatives. Using literature as a stimulus, teachers are encouraged to link the text with relevant math manipulatives in a hands-on, "minds-on" problem-solving learning environment.

The first six chapters of *Math Memories You Can Count On* provide the framework for implementing a literature-based approach in teaching math. Chapter 1: Memories of Mathematics Instruction focuses on the importance of building positive math memories that lead to productive math attitudes over a lifetime. Chapter 2: Creating Positive Math Memories focuses on creating a positive problem-solving learning environment. Chapter 3: Building New Mathematics Memories outlines the literature-based approach to teaching mathematics and details its benefits in a mathematics program. Chapter 4: Securing Long-Lasting Math Memories provides suggestions for selecting, organizing, and implementing literature in the primary classroom. Reflecting on Whitin's words: "Pigeonholing books with grade indexes can actually hinder learning," I looked beyond grade-level labels in choosing high interest-level books for primary students. (Whitin, David. May 2002. "The Potentials and Pitfalls of Integrating Literature into the Mathematics Program." *Teaching Children Mathematics.*) Teachers who know and listen to their students are the best judges of what books will be helpful to them. Chapter 5: Exploring Meaningful Math Memories discusses the appropriate math manipulatives and their usage and linkages to the literature. Chapter 6: Investigating Appropriate

Using different forms of children's literature helps teachers accommodate the different learning styles of their students and strengthen their communication skills while addressing the key mathematical skills and concepts in meaningful contexts.

— Early Math Strategy Report

Methods to Measure Growth in Math Understanding includes information about appropriate assessment and evaluation strategies, tools, and applications. Chapter 7: The Five Mathematics Strands explores the math strands one by one, providing specific suggestions for applicable literature, math manipulatives, and sample activities evolving from the storyline. Most of the activities are designed for independent explorations and are well suited for students to work on cooperatively in small groups. The directions are addressed to teachers. The book concludes with a Final Note of encouragement to teachers using the literature-based approach, followed by two appendices that provide a bibliography of children's literature and professional literature. A final appendix supplies four reproducible graphic organizers for teacher use in implementing the literature-based approach.

The literature has been chosen and grouped to relate to the five math strands:

- Number Sense and Numeration
- Measurement
- Geometry and Spatial Sense
- Patterning and Algebra
- Data Management and Probability

Each strand is organized around Big Ideas (key mathematical concepts), and the strands are interconnected. The interconnections between knowledge, skills, and concepts strengthen children's understanding of mathematical content and processes within and across each strand. Integrating literature and math in a meaningful context is a powerful key to understanding the complexities of math and its application in our world. The graphic below is an example of how children's literature provides a meaningful context for understanding the concept of time.

Focus: Measurement Strand
Summary: Hutchins explains the concept of time, from seconds to hours, on both analog and digital clocks, from years to millennia on the calendar.
Connecting Strands: Number Sense and Numeration
Connecting Big Idea (Key Concept): Fractions
Background Information
In telling time, children must relate halves and fourths to parts of a circle. Teacher-made or commercial circles are good models for connecting fractions to telling time on the analog clock.

—Friederwitzer & Berman

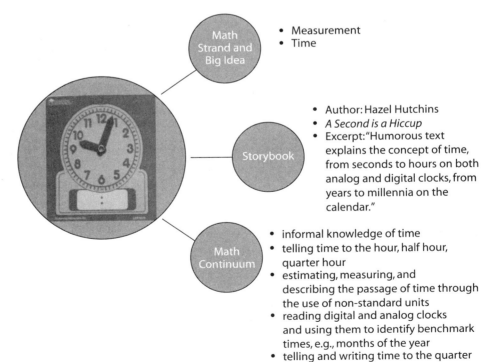

Math Strand and Big Idea
- Measurement
- Time

Storybook
- Author: Hazel Hutchins
- *A Second is a Hiccup*
- Excerpt: "Humorous text explains the concept of time, from seconds to hours on both analog and digital clocks, from years to millennia on the calendar."

Math Continuum
- informal knowledge of time
- telling time to the hour, half hour, quarter hour
- estimating, measuring, and describing the passage of time through the use of non-standard units
- reading digital and analog clocks and using them to identify benchmark times, e.g., months of the year
- telling and writing time to the quarter hour using digital and analog clocks
- reading time using analog clocks to the nearest 5 minutes

Cluster of Books Related to the Concept of Time

Burns, Marilyn. *This Book Is About Time*
Carle, Eric. *The Very Hungry Caterpillar*
Carle, Eric. *The Grouchy Ladybug*
Gleick, Beth. *Time Is When*
Gold, Kari Jenson. *It's Time!*
Hutchins, Pat. *Clocks and More Clocks*
Maestro, Betsy. *The Story of Clocks and Calendars*
Older, Jules. *Telling Time: How to Tell Time on Digital and Analog Clocks!*

Math is everywhere!

There are many ways to use books to ensure that children are afforded as many opportunities as possible to do math both inside and outside the classroom.

Throughout *Math Memories You Can Count On*, you will find reviews and recommendations for children's literature you can use in each of the five math strands. After reading this book and implementing its suggestions, I'm sure it won't be long before you discover that using children's literature offers an easy, effective instructional strategy in your primary mathematics program.

1   Memories of Mathematics Instruction

Reflecting on Real Math Memories

Many teachers feel that they have limited math backgrounds; yet, math is a skill we all use throughout our lives. Current research indicates that "past experiences affect how teachers teach." (Presto, Kevin and Corey Drake. Dec. 2004/Jan. 2005. *Teaching Children Mathematics.*) Many teachers have less than fond memories of math. These negative memories can lead to a lack of confidence and a sense of insecurity in teaching math. "Limits in confidence and comfort limit practice." (McDuffie, Amy. 2004. "Mathematics Teaching as a Deliberate Practice: An Investigation of Elementary Pre-service Teacher's Reflective Thinking During Student Teaching." *Journal of Mathematics Teacher Education.*)

I've been fortunate to work with and observe many teachers teaching mathematics at all grade levels. I've reflected on their math experiences and observed the impact of their teaching on their students' attitudes and achievement in mathematics. Recent study data indicate a positive correlation between attitude and achievement in mathematics. (*Early Math Strategy, The Report of the Expert Panel on Early Math in Ontario,* 2003.) If teachers have a positive attitude toward math teaching and learning, then it is more than likely their students will achieve at a higher level in mathematics. Likewise, teachers who have negative attitudes toward math teaching and learning will be more likely to see their students achieve at a lower level in math.

If the way we teach mathematics to students in the 21st-century classroom is to change for the better, then we need to investigate where we are on the teaching and learning mathematics continuum and how we can move ahead to create positive learning climates for effective teaching for all students.

In my work with pre-service elementary teachers, we spend a great deal of time reflecting on our mathematics histories. One of my student teachers' first tasks is to create their own math stories. Students reflect on these math memories throughout their years of formal schooling.

A Pre-Service Teacher's Math History

This math autobiography written by a future teacher illustrates the powerful effect that early life experience can have on teachers of mathematics.

My Math Autobiography Memories

My mathematics career is one of mostly shrinking numbers. In early elementary years, I participated in math classes with some excitement but was never keen on them. One of my Grade 2 report cards indicates that my math skills were average and that my teacher saw "no significant difficulties" with basic addition and subtraction functions. However, I recall having some difficulty with simple addition and subtraction back then. It's a trait that exists today, and one that has led to an inability to grasp mathematics concepts completely.

I think the downward turning point in my math career came in Grade 6, when I really struggled with complex calculations. I remember the year well because I had a teacher with whom I just didn't click. About halfway through the semester, I was put into the math remedial group, which meant I had a few more questions to do each night for homework. Knowing what I know now about extra support and positive work environments in school, I can see that the remedial group was probably doomed to be ineffective. Simply having more math problems to solve each night was not what I required.

My math abilities recovered somewhat in Grade 8. Again, I was placed in a remedial group, but this time the group met during class to sort out problems before taking work home. This proved to be a much better system, and one that resulted in me scoring a B in Grade 8 math. The euphoria of my math success, however, faded quickly when I got to high school. Grade 9 math proved difficult; my first attempt resulted in a D. I took the course again and significantly improved my mark. I am certain this happened because my teacher was so dedicated to assisting me. She had me stay after class a few nights a week with a small group of students to work on extra problems and share ideas with her. I appreciated her efforts and, in turn, earned a B in the course.

Grade 10 math, however, was a proverbial nightmare. I dropped out of the class after failing the first two unit tests. I ended up picking up the credit in the second semester, but just barely. After the Grade 10 debacle, I ceased pursuing advanced-level math credits and enrolled in general-level courses. I did well in these courses, but since they were not OAC math prerequisites, my official math career ended in Grade 12.

As I look back, it's easy to see that the years I did well in math happen to coincide with years in which I had an effective instructor. The teachers who spent time with me, ensuring that I understood math processes, managed to get the most out of my skills. I think I'll take this knowledge with me to my math classrooms. I realize how difficult math can be and, what's most important, I realize how an effective, caring math teacher can make a difference.

Bar Graph to show the Teacher's Mathematical Performance and Attitude toward Mathematics (Adapted from research by Guillaume & Kirtman) ■ = Math Enjoyment, ▨ = Math Achievement

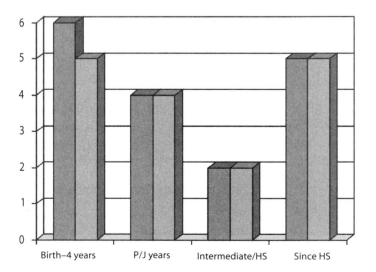

Teachers' beliefs and practices are shaped by years of experience with math as students in school and beyond.

— Ball & Mewborn

When I reflect on my pre-service teachers' mathematics stories, it's easy to observe a correlation between attitude and achievement in mathematics. If teachers have negative experiences as students of math, these experiences can impede their use of math in the classroom. It's only natural that teachers tend to emphasize subjects that they are more comfortable teaching.

Research on children's learning in the first six years of life validates the importance of early experiences in mathematics for lasting positive outcomes. (*NCTM News Bulletin*, Jan./Feb. 2008.) Children's stories give insight into their beliefs about how best to teach mathematics. Because a solid base of mathematical understanding is developed in the first few years of school (McCain & Mustard, 1999.) effective instruction in mathematics in the primary grades is crucial. Further, Kamii notes, "Young students are building beliefs about what math is, about what it means to know and do math and about themselves as math learners. These beliefs influence their thinking, performance attitudes, and decisions about studying math in later years." (Kamii, 2000.) It's critical for teachers to find a way to teach math that fosters positive attitudes in children toward learning math. Connecting children's literature with hands-on math manipulatives is an engaging and effective instructional approach to teaching mathematics. Children's literature can capture students' interest and stimulate their imagination. High-quality, well-designed children's books help students build bridges from the concrete to the abstract while motivating them to learn math.

Since young children's earliest experiences come through solving problems and communicating their responses, we need to create a positive learning environment that nurtures problem solving and values a variety of ways of communicating the message (talking, writing, drawing, and so on).

2   Creating Positive Math Memories

The Mathematics Learning Environment

Problem solving is natural to young children because the world is new to them, and they exhibit curiosity, intelligence, and flexibility as they face new situations. The challenge is to build on children's innate problem-solving inclinations and to preserve and encourage a disposition that values problem solving.

— Trafton & Midgett

Many people learned mathematics procedures first and then solved word problems after practicing to recite the number facts and carry out number operations by rote. This information was transmitted from the teacher to students.

— *Facilitator's Handbook: A Guide to Effective Instruction in Mathematics, K–6*

Teacher's actions are what encourage students to think, question, solve problems and discuss their ideas, strategies and solutions.

— *Principles and Standards for School Mathematics*

While we as educators are aware of how children learn, there is uncertainty around what constitutes an optimal mathematics-learning environment in today's primary classrooms.

Mathematics reform ushered in *"problem solving"* and *"ongoing communication"* as key components of all effective mathematics learning. Unlike rote learning, teaching and learning mathematics through problem solving and the development of conceptual understanding encourages students to reason their way to a solution or a new understanding. Many elementary teachers continue to feel uneasy creating a problem-solving environment, rich in dialog, where "real" mathematics knowledge and understanding can take place. Instead, they opt for a more traditional environment, focusing solely on textbooks and worksheets. Convinced they do not have a strong "mathematics background," these teachers employ methods many of us may recognize: low-level questioning, fill-in-the-blank activity sheets, and show-and-tell vignettes. As Ritchhart states, "In the face of enormous opportunity, many teachers either look back to what they had done previously or look to what others are doing, rather than look forward to what can give students real power." (Ritchhart, Ron. April 1999. "Generative Topics: Building a Curriculum Around Big Ideas." *Teaching Children Mathematics*.)

Research has shown that many children are unready to comprehend abstract concepts until they reach a certain stage of intellectual development. Perhaps there was and still is minimal understanding of the subject that has forced teaching methods to remain relatively stagnant. Lack of time, lack of resource materials (both print and non-print), lack of confidence in the subject matter, and lack of familiarity with math teaching methodologies are just some of the barriers to creating change in mathematics classrooms for the 21st century. Sadly, these obstructions create an environment in which children are not encouraged to ask their own questions and provide alternative solutions to problems. Such hidebound classrooms fall short of establishing the kinds of learning environments proposed by educational philosophers such as Herbert Spencer, Rousseau, and others—environments that *accompany* children rather than lead them in the search for knowledge.

The future of math teaching in the primary grades depends on how well we can make this shift. It begs the question: "What makes an effective mathematics learning environment?"

Developing a Mathematically Literate Problem-Solving Environment

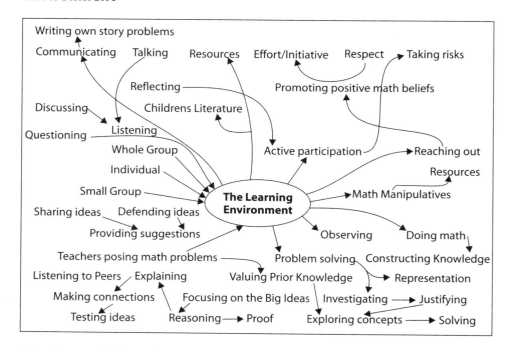

The characteristics embedded in the learning environment mindscape above demonstrate a shift in the culture of the mathematics primary classroom. In this environment, students and teachers listen carefully to each other, respond to each other, and pose questions to each other. The teacher is now a partner of the larger mathematical learning community.

Ball states, "the teacher needs a bifocal perspective—perceiving the math through the mind of the learner while perceiving the mind of the learner through math." (Ball, Deborah. 1993. "Halves, Pieces and Twoths: Constructing Representational Contexts in Teaching Fractions." *Teaching Children Mathematics*.)

Using children's literature to pose a variety of problems drawn from real-life experiences helps teachers move from direct instruction to inquiry-style instruction where students discover properties of numbers and relationships. Math-related children's literature allows children to:

- bring their own background of experiences to the text
- extend their understanding of concepts and skills in a problem-solving environment, and more

Teachers who feel uncomfortable teaching math can ease into using the literature to pose open-ended problems, allowing students to construct their own math leaning and understanding. Building on previous experiences, teachers can provide learning opportunities using literature as a springboard for helping students understand math concepts in meaningful contexts.

Promoting Problem-Solving Skills in the Math Classroom Using Children's Literature

Children's literature as a context for problem-posing investigations is a wonderful way to support problem-solving learning. Books act as high-interest word problems for children. Teachers can pose rich mathematics problems by basing scenarios on stories from children's literature. Researchers in the field identify the following elements common to problem solving: a series of steps, usually starting with a definition of the problem; a degree of creativity in suggesting possible solutions; selection of a solution; execution of the solution; and evaluation of the results. Stories provide a vehicle for teaching the steps implicit in the problem-solving process. *If I Built a Car* by Chris Van Dusen provides insight into a mathematician's habits of mind (curiosity, creativity, persistence, imagination, initiative, open-mindedness, risk taking) and focuses on the problem-solving process. In Dusen's story, Jack describes the kind of car he would build—one with amazing accessories and with the capability of travelling on land, in the air, and on and under the sea. Jack designs the ultimate fantasy car. Inspired by zeppelins, trains, Cadillacs, and old planes—with brilliant colors and shiny chrome—he creates an incredible image. Robert the Robot starts up the engine and Jack and his dad set off on a wacky test-drive. Jack's imagination and creativity in designing the ideal car will engage both boys and girls.

Embodied in Dusen's story are these key elements of problem solving: a thinking strategy; use of critical and creative thinking skills; a means of analyzing a situation; a means of applying past experience and knowledge to the problem; a focus on reaching a specific goal; a series of steps in any given model; a recognition that steps are recursive. The teacher's role throughout the problem-solving process is to foster the use of mathematical processes that support effective learning. Problem solving is one of seven mathematical processes that support effective learning in mathematics. Students must ask questions, explore, reason, reflect, connect, represent (e.g., develop models and methods), provide proof, communicate, and select tools and computational strategies. Students acquire and apply mathematical knowledge and skills through these processes. Teachers can use *If I Built a Car* to introduce and discuss the steps in the problem-solving process. Dusen's book also lends itself naturally to developing students' attitudes about learning (e.g., perseverance, willingness to revise their thinking, and appreciation for the value of risk taking). Extend its use by organizing students into cooperative learning groups to focus on the following task: to identify, select, record, and present the elements of problem solving as outlined in the story.

Children's literature provides students the context for a variety of experiences to develop mathematical habits of mind and practice their problem-solving skills using different strategies (e.g., counting, modelling, different representations—concrete to symbolic). The goal is for students to learn to reason through situations and develop a problem-solving schema that is effective for them. Stories promote patterns of cause and effect and problem solutions that encourage children to look for a pattern and employ a number of problem-solving strategies to include: guessing and checking, using objects, acting out the problem, drawing a picture, constructing a table, writing an equation, making models, and so on. Further, stories provide a model for students to recognize the elements of effective decision-making.

To provide the necessary hands-on linkage with the literature, follow the reading and discussion of Dusen's *If I Built a Car* with the introduction of

Multilink blocks (Cubes, Quadrants, Prisms, and Isos). Allow children playtime for the exploration of the different types of blocks and their function. Reflect on best practices—introducing mathematics concepts in a problem-solving context —and pose a problem that evolves from the story to challenge students to build a vehicle using the math manipulative Multilinks. This activity provides a natural entry point for students to familiarize themselves with the use and function of the manipulative, thus reinforcing the use of objects as a key problem-solving strategy. Students discover, for example, that when four Quadrants fuse together, they create a wheel, leading to a more efficient functioning model. The more familiar they are with the manipulatives, the more confident students become in their usage. The same can be said about most tools and their usage in helping students find solutions and, ultimately, solve problems.

Quality Children's Literature as a Springboard to Developing Problem-Solving Skills in Mathematics

Children's literature cuts across a variety of reading levels, inviting students at different grade levels within the primary division to pose their own questions evolving from the storyline at their own developmental level. Teachers can use the following selection of literature for this purpose.

1. *MATH-terpieces—The Art of Problem-Solving* by Greg Tang underscores the importance of four basic rules in problem solving, with the goal of teaching children to be more systematic in their approach to problem solving. Tang's charming rhyming text provides information about the artist and poses a mathematical challenge to group objects in various ways, for example, "April Showers," in which Tang features a Renoir painting titled *The Umbrella* and asks readers to group different numbers of umbrellas to make nine. While introducing students to art history, the book also manages to help them hone their understanding of addition and learn higher-level thinking skills while practicing their creative problem-solving skills.

2. *Math for All Seasons* by Greg Tang poses problems as riddles in the context of infectious rhymes that span the seasons. He encourages children to think creatively by looking for patterns and recognizing groupings. A first-rate book to use when developing problem-solving skills and tactics. Rhyming verses and illustrations pose number problems that students must solve using creative methods.

   Tang further encourages children to keep an open mind and use creativity and common sense to solve problems in new and unexpected ways rather than through formulas and memorization.

3. *Math Curse* by Jon Scieszka
   The math curse begins on a Monday when a math teacher tells the class that they can think of almost *everything* as a math problem. From then on, nearly every event constitutes a math problem. In this engaging story, a child views her everyday activities, such as selecting clothes, catching the bus, and more, as one mathematics problem after another. Scieszka challenges the reader to view life as a math problem by applying different math principles to everyday issues, like telling time, dividing food into equal portions, counting

objects, and so on. The book is packed full of math concepts all presented in the context of everyday circumstances. Many math story problems on each page challenge children to find solutions and solve problems. The illuminating message of *Math Curse* is: *Math is all around us.*

4. *Solve It!* by **Jennifer Osborne** uses simple, math-related language and visuals in the context of text and illustrations to provide meaningful clues that empower children to solve problems effectively. Osborne's clever use of rhyming text and higher-level questioning challenges children to think through and find solutions to the problems posed. Numerous questions provide opportunities for students to engage in the habits of mind akin to a mathematician's.

5. *The Best of Times* by **Greg Tang** underscores the importance of four basic rules in problem solving: keeping an open mind, looking for unusual number combinations, using multiple skills (like subtracting to add), and looking for patterns. This book brilliantly reinforces habits of mind of effective math problem-solvers and helps children become more systematic in their approach to problem solving.

Promoting Communication Skills in the Math Classroom Using Children's Literature

A second math-related process skill with which one can utilize children's literature is communication. Problem solving and communication are closely linked to all the other mathematical processes. Communication is the process of expressing mathematical ideas and understanding orally, visually, and in writing—using numbers, symbols, pictures, graphs, diagrams, and words. (*The Ontario Curriculum: K–8.*)

Mathematics is a means of communication. Encouraging young children to use pre-writing or picture drawing with words, to include telling and discussing what happened using vocabulary, expression, and recalling events, are all part of verbal and written communication in mathematics classrooms. Students are charged with expressing their ideas clearly while mastering basic skills and concepts and solving problems. Children's literature involving mathematics creates a natural context for talking about math.

Reflecting on the storyline in Dusen's *If I Built a Car,* you can encourage students to take part in related class or group discussions, use manipulative materials, and/or keep a journal to communicate their learning. These experiences give students the opportunity to see the relationship of language to concepts and ideas in a problem-solving learning environment. "Teachers of Mathematics highlight the importance of giving students opportunities to use and discuss multiple representations during problem solving." (NCTM, 2000.)

Designing and building models of cars, a logical outgrowth of *If I Built a Car,* naturally leads children to discuss and share their experiences. When students go through the process of designing and making models of cars, they have multiple opportunities to engage in rich dialog. As teachers, we need to tap into this opportunity and encourage and guide our students to engage in mathematical discourse.

Talking does not merely reflect thought, but it generates new thoughts and new ways to think. As members of a collaborative learning community, the children are learning that together they can go further than any of them could go alone.

—Lev Vygotsky

To be mathematically literate, students need to develop and express their math thinking through verbal and written communication. Reading, listening, drawing, giving oral explanations, writing descriptions, using tables and charts and using manipulatives are at work in this problem-solving environment.

—NCTM, 1998

Talking, drawing and writing can give students the opportunity to justify their thinking, formulate questions, and summarize important insights. Drawing and writing freeze ideas so that learners can return to them for reflection, refinement, discussion, and amendment.

— Whitin & Whitin

Communication skills are interconnected, beginning with oral language and continuing to computing. Each language form processes information differently; for example, graphs can represent our learning. Communication vehicles such as multimedia, computers, personal contact, and books allow appropriate communication to take place. Teachers can provide the necessary encouragement and support students need to develop their mathematical communication skills by creating opportunities to practice these skills. Working in small groups, in pairs, and individually allows greater opportunities to develop students' ideas, address their misconceptions, and learn to communicate their reasoning.

Children's literature in the primary classroom is a wonderful medium for strengthening ongoing communication skills in mathematics. The National Council of Teachers of Mathematics emphasizes the significant role of communication in helping children construct understandings of math concepts and develop connections between their informal knowledge and the abstract symbolism of math concepts. (Hunsader, Pat. 2004. "Mathematics Trade Books: Establishing Their Value and Assessing Their Quality." *The Reading Teacher.*)

Books such as Judy Nayer's *More or Less?* introduce vocabulary common to all mathematics classrooms (e.g., *more, less, fewer*). Teachers can use this big book as a read-aloud to introduce relevant vocabulary in the context of inquiry. Questions such as *Which building has fewer windows?* and *Which building has many more?* challenge students to think about the meaning of the words related to mathematics. Teachers can extend students' learning by encouraging them to work in small groups to create their own mathematics vocabulary big book. Display the book in the mathematics corner in the classroom. This is an excellent way to engage students in meaningful learning experiences that afford an opportunity to represent their learning.

Children's literature represents all the mathematics strands, and these same opportunities to develop a deeper understanding of mathematics vocabulary are apparent. For example, Cindy Neuschwander introduces vocabulary relevant to the Geometry and Spatial Sense strand. Her book *Sir Cumference and the Sword in the Cone—A Math Adventure* introduces math vocabulary (e.g., *radius, vertex*) in the context of story. As well, students are inspired to learn about 3-D shapes in the world of Geometry. Neuschwander deftly uses text and illustrations to engage students in hands-on explorations using such relevant math manipulatives as wood/foam geometric solids. Make the folding geometric solids accessible for students. Encourage students to use the folding geometric shapes to create the shapes introduced in the book (cube, pyramid, rectangular prism, triangular prism). Extend their learning by encouraging students to create 3-D shapes beyond the models embedded in the text.

For opportunities beyond the text, provide a hands-on technology experience in which students work on the computer with virtual manipulatives. Note that virtual representations of concrete manipulatives are just like the pictures in the books. They can be manipulated in the same ways a concrete manipulative can.

Using children's literature to develop an understanding of math vocabulary is one way to strengthen communication skills. You can also draw on children's stories to provide meaning around the complexities of mathematical concepts. For example, Miriam Schlein's *More Than One* effectively explores the concept of "one." Schlein explains how the number one can refer to a single item, the two shoes in a pair, the seven days in a week, the twelve eggs in a dozen, all the trees in a forest, and much more. Throughout the text, thought-provoking questions such as "Can ONE be different, different every time?" engage students in mean-

The ability to manipulate the visual representation, or object, on the computer connects the user with the real teaching and learning power of virtual manipulatives, that is, the opportunity to make meaning and see relationships as a result of one's own actions.

— Moyer, Bolyard & Spikell

ingful discussion. Encourage students to work in small groups in discussing Schlein's questions to come to a meaningful understanding of the concept of "one." Have each group present their findings to the whole class.

Quality Children's Literature as a Springboard to Developing Communication Skills in Mathematics

1. *Short, Tall, Big, or Small?* **by Kari Gold** affords students the opportunity to extend their understanding of mathematical vocabulary in relation to size through meaningful text and illustrations. Brief questions such as "Who's short? Who's tall? Who's heavy? Who's light?" encourage students to observe, think, and compare animal photos in the big-book format. Use a "think-pair-share" activity to provide many opportunities for students to get together to discuss their choices. To extend student's learning and encourage oral communication, conduct a walk around the schoolyard. Encourage students to find objects in nature that lend themselves to size comparison (e.g., rocks, leaves). Snap digital photos of found objects, e.g., light and heavy, big and small. Display in a photo gallery to represent students' mathematical learning.

2. *Parts of a Whole* **by Kari Gold** is a charming read-aloud that reinforces a deeper understanding of mathematical relationships regarding fractions. Gold's rhyming text, highlighted key fraction-related vocabulary, powerful illustrations, focused questions, and leading hands-on applications make this an excellent choice for your collection. Gold's spotlight on food creates meaningful understanding and heightens children's desire to communicate with one another. Oral communication centres logically around the meaning of concepts: part, whole, half, same, equal. Use manipulatives to create a more meaningful understanding of fractions (whole, parts) as a natural connection of the text and hands-on activities. Manipulatives could include teacher/student-prepared, commercial, and/or virtual manipulatives. Provide lots of time for students to explore and investigate the hands-on materials.

3. *Tally O'Malley* **by Stuart J. Murphy** is a book I have recommended for use in the Data Management and Probability strand. Representing is one of the communication skills we need to develop in our students, and Murphy does this well. On a car trip to the beach, the O'Malley children compete by playing games. They use a tally chart to keep score. Visuals tallying up the points throughout the story provide an excellent demonstration of how to collect, organize, and display data using tally charts. Offer many opportunities for students to gather data to answer a question, using a simple survey with a limited number of responses, e.g., *What is your favorite pet?* Encourage students to present their findings.

4. *You Can't Buy a Dinosaur with a Dime* **by Harriet Ziefert** is a terrific introduction on how money works in today's society. Ziefert includes a host of hands-on activities at the back of the book, providing students many opportunities to work with money. Pose problems and have students pose

problems that encourage the use of money. Use coin and bill sets and money stamps to provide hands-on experiences. Have students work in groups to solve the problems. Extend students experiences with money by forging a home-school partnership. Work with students to list common jobs around the house. Ask students to decide what each job would be worth. Have individual students keep track of the jobs they do and add up the money they earned for the week. Invite students to share their money experiences.

Children's math-related literature can build communication skills and provide opportunities for the development of problem-solving skills. Indeed, children's literature presents an overall context for a wide variety of experiences for students to demonstrate the "habits of a mathematician": problem solving, communication, reasoning, and making connections.

Chapter 3 focuses on the literature-based approach as a vital strategy for teaching mathematics and outlines the many advantages of using children's literature in primary classrooms.

3 Building New Mathematics Memories

The Literature-Based Approach to Teaching Mathematics

Literacy infusion works especially well in the younger grades, but this class has also taught me that, no matter what age you are, effectively written children's literature can engage learners. This approach greatly assisted my lesson-plan writing obligations for this class. I found that creating an effective lesson plan is much easier when you begin with an idea for infusing literacy in the lesson. I created a math sentence-writing lesson, which included a read-aloud of a great math book called *Twenty Is Too Many*, which teaches subtraction sentence-writing through the eyes of twenty guinea pigs on a boat. When I implemented this lesson, I found that the students were fully engaged in the story. During practice time, I was also able to refer back to the literature to check for student understanding. Not only can a good story regroup and refocus the class but it can also provide practical formative assessment opportunities for teachers.

—Reflections of a prospective teacher

Storytelling can be a vital part of a classroom culture of problem solving.

—Lewis, Long & MacKay

There are many teaching strategies from which to choose to teach mathematics in the primary grades with success. *Math Memories You Can Count On* uses a literature-based approach to teaching mathematics, concentrating on key mathematical concepts (Big Ideas) and the knowledge and skills that go with those concepts. The specific mathematical skills inherent in each strand have been grouped to reflect the Big Ideas to encourage a deeper understanding of the key math concepts. The mathematical content and processes are embedded in the literature of the five strands: Number Sense and Numeration, Geometry and Spatial Sense, Measurement, Patterning and Algebra, and Data Management and Probability.

I have made every attempt to reinforce mathematical concepts using the literature through a problem-solving context. "Not all mathematics instruction can take place in a problem solving context. Certain aspects of mathematics need to be taught explicitly. Mathematical conventions including the use of mathematical symbols and terms are one such aspect and they should be introduced to students as needed to enable them to use the symbolic language of mathematics." *(A Guide to Effective Instruction in Mathematics.)* Concept books provide excellent support for this venture, and they have been interwoven throughout *Math Memories You Can Count On*.

Many teachers have a strong language arts background, and the literature-based approach to teaching mathematics in this book uses their strength in language to strengthen literacy and numeracy skills and concepts in a balanced mathematics program. The use of literature in the mathematics program naturally affords multiple opportunities for students to communicate through talk with their peers and teachers.

With the focus now on mathematics as thinking and reasoning, making connections, solving problems, and communicating ideas, we need to look for best practices that can help us meet with success in our mathematical understanding. Using math-related literature is an effective strategy to teach the Big Ideas. Using this strategy allows children to bring their own background of experiences to the text and extend their understanding of concepts and skills in the classroom. This understanding transfers and extends naturally in the home. When teachers use literature in math instruction, the benefits are twofold. Literacy is encouraged and math is at the frontline. An emphasis on numerous print and non-print resources minimizes the use of traditional textbooks. Children are encouraged to ask questions and, through investigating, exploring, and manipulating materials, reach a better understanding of mathematical concepts. Activities evolve from the literature and are initiated through guided teacher prompts rather than recycled teacher-designed questions. The focus is on understanding and applying concepts. This language-based approach to mathematics instruction helps teachers apply their language arts skills, linking them to children's mathematics learning.

Benefits of Using Literature in a Math Program

There are very many benefits to choosing math-related literature as an effective strategy to teach mathematics in primary classrooms. Following are just a few of these benefits.

Math-related literature introduces math concepts and skills through the language and illustrations within the context of story.

A Million Dots by Andrew Clement

MATH FOCUS: Large Numbers

BIG IDEA (KEY CONCEPT): Concept of one million

This is a wonderful book for teaching children to understand the concept of one million. Clement begins with a question that causes any child to wonder if he or she really knows what a million looks like. Throughout the book, Clement continually probes his audience to think about a million via questions, supportive text, and illustrations. Each page features a random dot number that Clements uses as a background for self-imposed images. The idea of a million dots running throughout the entire book is very appealing to children. Children are simply fascinated with big numbers and engaged in learning the interesting facts Clement frequently shares, e.g., *"It would take eleven and a half days to count each dot, one by one."*

Math-related literature helps children to develop their imagination through exploring and investigating math principles.

When asked how to help a child who was gifted in math, Einstein answered, "Read him the great myths of the past. Stretch his imagination." One of the goals of establishing an effective elementary math program is building an environment open to inquiry and supportive of imagination.

Riddle-iculous MATH by Joan Holub

MATH FOCUS: Factors, Measurement, Fractions, Multiplication

Holub includes riddles, math problems, and jokes in a rhyming, ridiculous way. Poems, stories, illustrations, and drawings come together to tap into any child's imagination. The humor in the illustrations sets children immediately at ease while they are engaged in learning mathematics. Throughout the book, Holub shares different vignettes followed by probing questions reinforcing the habits of a mathematician in a mathematics problem-solving learning environment. Any anxiety about learning mathematical skills and concepts is quickly forgotten. Children are inspired to write their own jokes/riddles using correct mathematics. *"The process of writing and solving riddles provides a rich context for learning new mathematical vocabulary."* (Sherrill, Carl. March 2005. "Math Riddles: Helping Children Connect Words and Numbers." *Teaching Children Mathematics.* NCTM.)

Math-related literature encourages integration with other subject areas.

While focusing on one topic, many children's books offer insight and knowledge of topics beyond their focus. A variety of activity-based experiences and focus on the Big Ideas that emerge from children's literature integrate math across the curriculum more effectively.

MATH-terpieces: The Art of Problem Solving by Greg Tang

MATH FOCUS: Problem Solving
BIG IDEA (KEY CONCEPT): Probability—combinations

This book teaches children the importance of four basic rules in problem solving: keeping an open mind, looking for unusual number combinations, using multiple skills (subtracting to add), and looking for patterns. Tang uses art history to expand his vision of creative problem solving, blending mathematics with art appreciation. One side of each two-page spread contains a colorful reproduction of a famous artwork and a poem that describes the painting or the artist. On the other side, Tang creates several different-sized groupings of elements from the artwork. He challenges children to create groups that add up to a certain number. Throughout the text, Tang introduces combinations, an important concept in probability, and challenges children to find patterns. Linkages of art and mathematics are embedded in this problem-solving learning environment.

Math-related literature provides teachers an opportunity to build knowledge and understanding of mathematical skills and concepts efficiently, raising a teacher's comfort level in teaching mathematics.

Teachers can quickly read fiction and non-fiction books on any math topic, in order to learn new information, reinforce existing knowledge, or extend their learning in preparation for planning mathematics opportunities in the classroom.

Can You Count to a Googol? by Robert Wells

MATH FOCUS: Large Numbers, Counting
BIG IDEA (KEY CONCEPT): Place Value

The text begins with one and increases by powers of 10 to a googol, the number represented by one followed by 100 zeros. This book provides a quick review for teachers around new ways of understanding place value. Teachers can home in quickly to learn new information and/or reinforce their existing knowledge of the mathematics concept. Wells provides a number of interesting ideas that may help teachers springboard into finding new instructional methods for introducing place value in a creative manner, instilling a new sense of children's understanding of the concept. Teachers are motivated to create hands-on opportunities for students.

Math-related literature provides multisensory experiences.

Specific children's books can introduce multisensory experiences. Auditory, visual, and tactile opportunities built naturally into the text draw children into the learning through their senses. Ideas presented in a non-threatening pictorial format benefit visual learners.

GRAPH IT! by Jennifer Osborne

MATH FOCUS: Graphing
BIG IDEA (KEY CONCEPT): Representation
SENSES: Auditory and Visual

This read-aloud big book contains relevant math text and corresponding representations of numbers in a wide variety of graphs (e.g., pictograph, bar graph, line graph). Osborne provides many opportunities for teachers to strengthen their students' auditory and visual senses. The colorful pictures and graphics draw children in and invite them to read along with the teacher, observe, listen, respond to the text and graphics, and pose their own questions. This read-aloud experience affords children numerous opportunities to extend their learning.

Ten Little Ladybugs by Melanie Gerth

MATH FOCUS: Counting
BIG IDEAS (KEY CONCEPTS): Counting on, Counting back
SENSE: Tactile

Another multisensory experience evolves quite naturally through the book *Ten Little Ladybugs*. Melanie Gerth's innovative thinking creates a wonderful tactile opportunity for all learners.

Ten colorful red, yellow, and orange plastic ladybugs are embedded in this book, providing an opportunity for children to interact with the text while being introduced to simple subtraction. Extensions that follow from the book may include opportunities for children to explore a variety of hands-on manipulatives used to support their understanding of concepts.

Math-related literature presents itself in a variety of book types and literary styles.

Children's literature encompasses a number of book types, as well as literary styles, including big books, story books, poetry books, discovery and exploration books, and more.

Using a variety of books that span the interest of every child offers many opportunities for children to succeed in building a better conceptual understanding of mathematics.

Math Potatoes by Greg Tang

MATH FOCUS: Problem Solving

Some children learn better when new material is introduced through poetry. The rhythm catches their attention, reinforcing their understanding of mathematical concepts. In *Math Potatoes*, Greg Tang combines math with poems and pictures to communicate in both verbal and visual ways.

By using the strategies embedded in his book, students can meet Tang's purpose, "To challenge kids to combine numbers in smart ways, not just obvious ways." Still other children find the singing and chanting inherent in some books helpful to their learning process.

Math-related children's literature ensures higher success in understanding math skills and concepts through reaching all developmental stages.

Children are at different developmental stages when they arrive at school. In developing concepts, each child has a different starting point that is determined by previous experiences and understanding. Whether he or she is in the very early stages of growth and development or in a more advanced stage, children's literature can enhance each child's understanding of math concepts at his or her level of development.

In meeting the needs of all children, traditional math textbooks cannot offer the same range as children's literature. With current emphasis on meeting the needs of all children, it is a priority to provide a wide variety of fiction and non-fiction materials from which children can select.

Children engage in and learn best when activities and literature match their stage of development. Teachers using children's literature as an approach to teaching mathematics are comfortable in knowing they can teach math effectively with the support of children's literature.

For example, we can use math-related literature to provide algebraic experiences that are developmentally appropriate and grow in difficulty. We can encourage our students to move along the growth continuum by providing them opportunities ranging from sorting objects by attributes to counting, reinforcing that the numbers are a pattern. Farther along the continuum, we can encourage students to observe that multiples of five end in five or zero, making another pattern. At the upper end of the growth continuum, we can encourage students to engage in making tessellations. *A Cloak for the Dreamer* **by Aileen Friedman** is an upper-end book that assists students in making and understanding tessellations.

What Comes Next? **by Kari Gold**
MATH FOCUS: Algebraic Understanding
BIG IDEA (KEY CONCEPT): Patterning

Gold asks relevant questions throughout this concept book to engage students in gaining a better understanding of patterning. The illustrations work with the text to reinforce student learning.

Math-related literature reinforces the importance of problem solving in mathematics classrooms.

Children's literature provides a meaningful problem-solving context emerging from math-related books.

Moira's Birthday **by Robert Munsch**
MATH FOCUS: Problem solving

Moira was supposed to have six children at her birthday party, but things got out of hand when she invited *all* the children in her school. How will Moira feed all of the children?

Math-related literature introduces the use of math manipulatives through text and illustrations.

Manipulatives are introduced naturally through children's literature, bridging the gap between concrete representations and abstract concepts. The introduction of math manipulatives encourages children to explore the use and function of hands-on materials that will enhance their understanding of math concepts and skills.

Grandfather Tang's Story by Ann Tompert

MATH FOCUS: Tangrams

This is an example of how text and illustrations can invite students to engage in learning. In partners, students can work with a set of tangram patterns and practice moving the pieces to create tangram animals. Vocabulary such as *slide, flip,* or *turn* is introduced in the context of the text and illustrations, enriching students' understanding of math concepts and skills.

Math-related literature provides a real-world feeling to mathematics.

Through text and illustrations, students are encouraged to draw meaningful connections between experiences in the classroom and life in the "real world."

Clocks and More Clocks by Pat Hutchins

BIG IDEA (KEY CONCEPT): Time

The main character in this story buys a multitude of clocks to place all over his house. The problem: they all tell different times. Hutchins encourages students to think about a time outside of school when knowing the correct time was important.

In making math-related literature a component of your primary classroom, the selection of the best math books is critical. Chapter 4 focuses on selecting, organizing, and implementing the literature based approach to teaching mathematics all in seven easy steps.

4 Securing Long-Lasting Math Memories

Useful books provide information, but stories have the magic in them that make you run out into the backyard at night and stare up into infinity to see what's there.

—Mark Twain. *The Adventures of Huckleberry Finn*

The Role of the Teacher

- Refer to the information in this chapter.
- Take along a copy of the criteria for selecting the best math books when you begin your search.
- Read the children's books yourself before choosing to use them in the classroom.
- Select books that will strengthen students' understanding of the mathematical processes in line with the Big Ideas.
- Think about real-world connections each book might offer for further class discussion.
- Become familiar with the "habits of mind" that mathematicians demonstrate, and search for books that will provide opportunities for students to model them as they do mathematics.

Selecting and Organizing the Literature

Familiarity with Twain's message helps us select fiction and non-fiction books that are entertaining, inviting, and exciting—books that grab children's attention. If you choose carefully, the excitement of discovery these books can generate is irreplaceable. Children gravitate naturally to exciting books.

The first step in your search is to become familiar with a wide variety of math-related children's literature, including fiction and non-fiction. As you read, remember the wisdom of C.S. Lewis when he says, "No book is really worth reading at the age of 10 which is not really worth reading at the age of 50."

When making your selections, employ a list of criteria to ensure your selection consists of the best math-related books for your primary classroom. Using these criteria helps to avoid a "watered-down" mathematics program. Fiction gives a unique perspective that allows children to know facts in another way, and to confirm what they are learning from informational sources. (Huck, 1987.)

You Can't Buy a Dinosaur with a Dime by Harriet Ziefert is an ideal example of the function and use of fiction in a literature-based math program. The rhyming text and bright, entertaining pictures introduce children to how money works in today's society. Ziefert leads children to respond to questions such as "Do you know how much you've saved if you haven't counted your money?" and "Can you spend without saving first?" This inquiring nature invites children to interact on a personal level with the text through such questions as "Have you spent money from your bank?" "How much?" and "How much do you have left?" As well, the book is an outstanding introduction to adding and subtracting small amounts of money. Ziefert concludes with a section on Money Fun. The author introduces children to data collected in a survey about allowances and gives interesting Facts About Money.

Non-fiction books provide accurate information that is consistent with current mathematics knowledge and understanding, thus reinforcing the Big Ideas uncovered in fiction.

The Money Book by Jennifer Osborne is full of beautiful, full-page, colorful, images inviting children to think about the value of money. Photos of Canadian currency, in both bills and coins, and graphic inserts help children think about the value of the dollar in pennies, nickels, dimes, and quarters. These types of experiences enrich children's understanding of the value of money and strengthen their knowledge and understanding of place value. Additionally, Osborne provides photos that demonstrate places in the community where knowing the value of money is key to interacting in the real world.

As you read children's literature, ask yourself the following questions. Your responses will help you choose the best books for encouraging mathematics teaching.

1. *Is there accuracy of content in the text and illustrations?*

Many children's books lend themselves to mathematics teaching and learning. Our task as teachers is to find them. Review the text, illustrations, and graphics first for their accuracy and secondly to determine the degree they address the mathematical processes, encourage problem-solving, and support the Big Ideas of mathematics content in the primary grades.

One Hundred Hungry Ants by Elinor Pinczes is an excellent example of fiction with a strong math thread woven throughout the narrative. It engages children in discussing the different ways in which the ants march (five rows of 20, ten rows of 10), counting to one hundred, and filling in the missing numbers in a Hundreds Chart. Opportunities leading to problem-solving experiences abound.

2. *Do the text and illustrations enhance mathematics concepts and skills?*

The skills developed through mathematics teaching help children make sense of their experiences. Children learn to observe, classify, seriate, communicate, measure, infer, predict, hypothesize, investigate, interpret, manipulate materials, and make models. Appropriate mathematics literature emphasizes these skills within the text and illustrations.

Non-fiction books such as *Great Estimations* by Bruce Goldstone and *Give It a Guess!* by Jennifer Osborne as well as fiction books like *Counting on Frank* by Rod Clement focus on developing the concept of estimation. Children engage in a number of skills: observing, measuring, communicating, predicting, hypothesizing, and manipulating materials.

3. *Do the book's mathematics and story complement each other?*

Mathematics should enhance what is already a good story. Margaret McNamara's *how many seeds in a pumpkin?* is a good example of mathematics and story working together. Charlie, the smallest child in his first grade class, discovers that the smallest pumpkin of the three the teachers bring to class is the one with the most seeds. Through hands-on investigation, Charlie solves a real math problem that evolves from the storyline.

4. *Does the text incorporate vocabulary familiar to mathematics teaching?*

Students can understand complex math vocabulary through books such as Jennifer Osborne's *Graph It!* that provide meaning in the context of text and detailed illustrations. Osborne introduces graphs, tally charts, pictographs, bar graphs, line graphs, metric measurement, circle graphs, and Venn diagrams. She encourages children to think, observe, and reflect on the specific features unique to each, using their knowledge and understanding of graphic organizers.

5. Is the book intellectually and developmentally appropriate?

Math content introduced within the story should be within one grade level of your audience. For example, a book like *Ten Little Ladybugs* by Melanie Gerth, which focuses on counting to 10 and back again, would be suitable for very young children. *A Million Dots* by Andrew Clements would be more developmentally appropriate for older children who have had experience in counting to 100 and beyond. Authors such as Stuart Murphy earmark their books to correlate to Grades 1 through 3.

6. Do the illustrations and text imply easy-to-use math manipulatives to help readers benefit from the mathematics knowledge and understanding embedded in the book?

Reading the literature carefully leads to a better understanding of the hands-on opportunities that can be extended to children to allow for exploration and investigation of the Big Ideas. Math manipulatives are key to children's understanding of math concepts and skills. The literature can direct children to explore and investigate mathematical problems using relevant concrete materials. Books such as *The Greedy Triangle* by Marilyn Burns, *Grandfather Tang's Story* by Ann Tompert, and *A Cloak for the Dreamer* by Aileen Friedman lend themselves well to encouraging the manipulation of tangram pieces, triangles, quadrilaterals, and polygons.

7. Have I chosen books that provide a balance in opportunities for all of the mathematics strands?

Selecting a wide variety of children's literature for mathematics teaching can be a positive experience for the classroom teacher. Place a strong emphasis on organizing the literature for classroom use. It should encourage easy access by both the students and the teacher. Good organization is critical to the success of the mathematics program.

One way to begin organizing is to establish a way to categorize the number of books that are relevant to one specific mathematics strand. You can place sticky letters (e.g., DM-Data Management) on the outside book cover. As you collect and categorize your books, work toward striking a balance among the five strands.

8. Do my selections reflect a variety of literary genres and vivid interesting writing styles that involve the children?

There are many kinds of math-related books. As you read these books randomly, make a conscious effort to include a variety of genres. Look for books that encourage math learning through rhyme, story, illustration, inquiry, and more. You may want to add additional categories.

9. Does the book facilitate real-world applications?

Books can facilitate the reader's involvement in and encourage the use and transfer of its mathematics to other situations. "When numbers and their operations are embedded in meaningful real-world contexts, children are able to make sense of mathematics, gain mathematical power, and develop a wider view of the place of mathematics in their world." (Reson, V.A.

"Principles and Standards for School Mathematics." NCTM, 2000.) Connecting mathematics to the real world is a priority when choosing children's literature to use in the classroom. For example, *What Comes in 2's, 3's & 4's?* by Suzanne Aker starts with the self (2 eyes, 2 ears) and moves on to the community, where children are encouraged to explore the real-world application of numbers: 2 ways to go on a seesaw, 3 leaves on poison ivy, and 4 seasons in the year.

Using the Literature in the Classroom

There is no one right way to organize the literature. Discovering your own way to organize is key to implementing successfully the literature and mathematics strategy. For example, developing text sets representing a wide variety of literary styles through the eye of a lens is one way to organize the literature in your classroom. *Math Memories You Can Count On* uses this organizational method connecting the literature and mathematics through a variety of lenses: Big Idea Lens, Literary Genre Lens, Author Lens, and Mathematical Process Lens. This is an easy method of ensuring that math is happening every day, everywhere!

Big Idea Lens

Literature plays an important role in supporting the development of the Big Ideas, or key math concepts, across the five math strands. Developing Big Idea text sets around key concepts is an easy way to organize the literature. Patterning, averaging, measuring, estimating, time, addition, and money are all examples of the key concepts embedded in the organizers specific to each strand. For example, the Big Ideas of counting, operational sense, quantity, relationships, and representation are embedded in the Number Sense and Numeration strand. In developing individual text sets around the Big Ideas, I like to use a variety of literature representing all the different genres while focusing on the key mathematical concepts.

Developing a Math-Related Text Set Through a Big Idea Lens

STRAND: Number Sense and Numeration
BIG IDEA: Quantity
KEY CONCEPT/SKILL: Money

MATH-RELATED LITERATURE SUGGESTIONS	GENRE
Axelrod, Amy. *Pigs Will Be Pigs*	Story
Brisson, Pat. *Benny's Pennies*	Story
Holtzman, Caren. *A Quarter from the Tooth Fairy*	Rhyme
Leedy, Loreen. *Monster Money Book*	Drama
Osborne, Jennifer. *The Money Book*	Big book (read-aloud)
Ziefert, Harriet. *You Can't Buy a Dinosaur with a Dime*	Problem solving

Literary Genre Lens

It is important to demonstrate using a variety of literary styles to meet the needs of all mathematics learners. *Math Memories You Can Count On* suggests selecting a variety of book types reflected in math-related children's books.

The Role of the Teacher
- Make math Big Idea collections accessible to students.
- Ensure math manipulatives are accessible to students.
- Begin sharing books with students that they enjoy and that interest them before teaching math concepts in the story.
- Read the story aloud and create an awareness of the linkage between literature and mathematics.
- Take advantage of the teachable moments.
- Activate students' prior knowledge.
- Pose questions and encourage students to pose their questions from the storyline.
- Provide opportunities to engage in open-ended discussions about the story.
- Provide opportunities for students to engage in practicing the mathematical processes and problem-solving skills.

Throughout this book, I have reviewed over 100 titles of the best math-related books representing a wide variety of literary styles for this purpose. In developing text sets around the Big Ideas using a specific book type (for example, story, rhyme/verse, big book), we can strengthen children's literacy skills while reinforcing their numeracy skills. Using stories as a vehicle to learn mathematics satisfies a child's curiosity and interest while introducing math concepts and skills in the context of story.

Developing a Math-Related Text Set Through a Literary Genre Lens

STRAND: Patterning and Algebra
BIG IDEAS: Finding, Describing, and Using Patterns
KEY CONCEPT/SKILL: Patterning

MATH-RELATED LITERATURE SUGGESTIONS	GENRE
Callella-Jones, Trisha. *Patterns All Around Me*	Storybook
Carle, Eric. *The Very Hungry Caterpillar*	Storybook
Carle, Eric. *Rooster's Off to See the World*	Storybook
Falconer, Elizabeth. *The House That Jack Built*	Storybook
Reid, Margarette. *The Button Box*	Storybook
Slobodkina, Esphyr. *Caps for Sale*	Storybook

Author Lens

Listening to or reading a good book allows us to think, reason, solve problems, compare and contrast, critique, and communicate in both old and new ways.

—Colin Ducolon

Become familiar with the works of the best math authors, many of whom I have identified within this book. Some authors whose works come to mind are Marilyn Burns, Amy Axelrod, Eric Carle, Kari Gold, Pat Hutchins, Loreen Leedy, Robert Munsch, Stuart Murphy, and Greg Tang. Many of these books have already been screened for authenticity and meet the criteria for selecting effective math-related books to augment your mathematics program.

In developing my author text sets, I begin by reflecting on my students' math needs, for example, problem solving. I look for an author or a group of authors that speak to this need and select books that represent a variety of literary styles. Having identified problem solving as a student need, I develop my author text set using, for example, Greg Tang's works. Tang deals with four basic rules for problem solving: keeping an open mind, looking for unusual number combinations, using multiple skills (like subtracting to add), and looking for patterns. In Tang's view, these will guarantee any child success in math.

Developing a Math-Related Text Set Through an Author Lens

STRAND: All five math strands
BIG IDEA: Problem Solving
KEY CONCEPTS/SKILLS: Fluctuate depending on the strand

MATH-RELATED LITERATURE SUGGESTIONS	GENRE
Tang, Greg. *The Best of Times*	Riddles
Tang, Greg. *The Grapes of Math*	Riddles
Tang, Greg. *Math Appeal*	Riddles
Tang, Greg. *Math for All Seasons*	Riddles
Tang, Greg. *Math Potatoes*	Riddles
Tang, Greg. *MATH-terpieces*	Riddles

Mathematical Process Lens

Mathematical processes—for example, problem solving, reasoning, proving, communicating, connecting, and representing—play a key role in developing students' conceptual understanding of math. Math-related literature supports the development of these processes. Developing individual text sets around the different processes helps students strengthen their knowledge, understanding, and application of the mathematical processes.

In developing the mathematical process of representation, children are naturally encouraged to interact with the many ways book types represent math in meaningful contexts. Graphic organizers, such as pictographs, bar graphs, and Venn diagrams; strategies, for example, tallies; and mathematical tools and illustrations all serve to help children know and understand math through the demonstration of a variety of ways to represent mathematics learning embedded in children's literature.

Developing a Math-Related Text Set Through a Process Lens

STRAND: All five math strands

BIG IDEA: Representation

KEY CONCEPTS/SKILLS: Fluctuate depending on the strand

MATH-RELATED LITERATURE SUGGESTIONS	GENRE
Axelrod, Amy. *Pigs in the Pantry*	Storybook
Carle, Eric. *Rooster's Off to See the World*	Storybook
Clements, Andrew. *A Million Dots*	Information
Murphy, Stuart. *Tally O'Malley*	Storybook
Osborne, Jennifer. *Graph It!*	Big book
Tompert, Ann. *Grandfather Tang's Story*	Storybook

Implementing the Literature-Based Approach to Teaching Mathematics

In successfully teaching mathematics in the primary grades, there are many teaching strategies from which to choose. As noted earlier, *Math Memories You Can Count On* uses a literature-based approach to teaching mathematics, linking children's literature with the mathematical skills and concepts. This resource demonstrates the use of children's literature in a number of ways: to introduce new vocabulary, to develop math concepts, to encourage the use of math manipulatives, to make connections with other concepts/disciplines, and/or to enrich and extend the concepts learned. To encourage a deeper understanding of the key concepts, I have grouped the specific mathematical skills inherent in each strand to reflect the Big Ideas related to each strand. The mathematical content and processes are embedded in the literature of the five math strands: Number Sense and Numeration, Measurement, Geometry and Spatial Sense, Patterning and Algebra, and Data Management and Probability.

I have attempted to present or reinforce mathematical concepts using the literature through a problem-solving context. Concept books are good to use to support this venture and references to them have been interwoven throughout this book.

Not all mathematics instruction can take place in a problem-solving context. Certain aspects of mathematics need to be taught explicitly. Mathematical conventions including the use of mathematical symbols and terms are one such aspect and they should be introduced to students as needed to enable them to use the symbolic language of mathematics.

— *Facilitator's Handbook: A Guide to Effective Instruction in Mathematics, K–6*

As noted previously, many teachers have a strong language arts background, and the literature-based approach in this book uses their strength in language to strengthen literacy and numeracy skills and concepts in a balanced mathematics program. The use of literature in the math program naturally affords multiple opportunities for students to communicate through talk with their peers and teachers. Children's books can be used as read-alouds, in math-centre activities, and/or in large-group, small-group, and individual learning.

I have included in this guide organizers such as flow charts, tables, and pictorial images to save teachers time in planning and to help them plan more effectively so that children are involved in doing mathematics. Organizers identify the related books, Big Idea text sets, math centres, math manipulatives, and assessment strategies for use in the primary classroom. The ultimate goal is to move all children toward understanding the Big Ideas—using children's books and hands-on discovery, exploration, and investigation activities embedded in a problem-solving context.

Getting Started – Seven Easy Steps

The following list summarizes the seven easy steps for implementing the literature-based approach to teaching mathematics.

1. Select a Mathematics Strand and Big Idea.
2. Review the expectations related to the Big Idea.
3. Cluster the expectations around the Big Idea.
4. Choose an appropriate assessment strategy (or strategies).
5. Search for the related literature.
6. Think of a problem using the literature as a catalyst.
7. Choose an instructional approach (guided math, shared math, independent math).

5   Exploring Meaningful Math Memories

Linking the Literature and Math Manipulatives

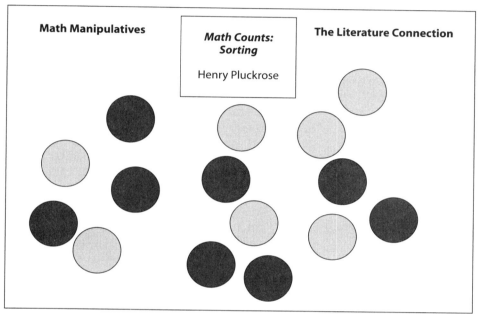

Two-Colored Counters (Commercial)—building mathematical understandings in counting

Students learn best when they are actively involved in using multiple senses and constructing understanding for themselves. That's why using a hands-on manipulative approach to mathematics is tremendously valuable for children in the primary grades. Cuisenaire rods, clocks, measuring tapes, dice, pattern blocks, dominoes—the choice of available manipulatives is endless. As teachers, we are challenged to:

- select concrete materials that support the Big Ideas
- help students bridge the gap between concrete and abstract functioning

Current research speaks to the significance of using manipulatives in the math classroom. To develop a true understanding of mathematical skills and concepts, students need continuous experience using manipulative materials in rich, structured investigations and instructional opportunities.

When introducing manipulatives, allow enough time for students to play freely and explore the appropriate manipulatives on their own, before engaging the students in a specific guided activity.

I'm often faced with this response when I speak to prospective and experienced teachers about the limited use of hands-on materials in primary classrooms: "I used to provide the students with math manipulatives, but they played with the materials so I took them away." When I probe deeper, I discover their misunderstandings around the use of math manipulatives and the developmental stages children naturally pass through from the concrete to the abstract. Young children find abstractions difficult to master. Allow seeing, touching, experimenting, and communicating to be integral components of a classroom environment where children are encouraged to engage in graphing, sorting, patterning, counting, estimating, and more. Indeed, the play stage is the first step in introducing primary students to the use of math manipulatives. As Burns suggests, whenever teachers are introducing a new manipulative, allow at least one math period for free exploration. When students have explored the materials on their own, they are more than ready for teachers to guide them in investigating some of the central concepts that support mathematics.

At this point, teachers can move on to developing inquiring questions such as, "Did you come close to your estimation?" "What if I add two to this pile?" and more. This can lead to creating specific interactive tasks for students to use the manipulatives. Allow numerous opportunities for students to probe for a deeper understanding of math concepts.

Linking hands-on math manipulatives with carefully selected books infused with mathematical thought provides students tactile experiences to help them model, describe, and explore mathematics. Books can introduce math manipulatives to children through text and illustrations. Some books are all-inclusive, containing a hands-on opportunity within the book. For example, *Ten Little Ladybugs* by Melanie Gerth is a board book with red, yellow, and orange plastic ladybugs embedded in its ten pages. Each page has cutouts so that, when you turn it, the ladybug on that page disappears but the others appear to move to the next spread. This engaging rhyming book teaches counting forwards to ten, counting backwards from ten, and simple subtraction with three-dimensional ladybugs.

Some books encourage the use of found materials as a strategy for getting hands-on materials into the classroom. Using found materials teaches children to protect our environment by practicing the "five Rs"—Reduce, Reuse, Recycle, Reinvent, Refuse. A book that comes to mind here is *Math Counts: Sorting* by Henry Pluckrose. Through text and illustrations, Pluckrose introduces and reinforces the need for counters, beads, buttons, seashells, seeds, marbles, and more found materials that help children solve mathematical tasks. *Sorting* introduces mathematical vocabulary (e.g., *set, sort*) alongside pictorial representations of found materials. For example, a full-page spread of buttons inspires students to sort found materials (in this case, buttons) into a set, making a set of buttons strengthening the understanding of math language in the context of the text.

Other books provide instructions for do-it-yourself manipulatives that lead students and teachers to make their own hands-on materials (e.g., card games). In this way, children become active partners in collecting, making, and organizing materials for use in the mathematics classroom, thus instilling a sense of pride in their work. At little or no cost, manipulatives are plentiful and easily accessible. The do-it-yourself method has been around for decades. With little effort, children can make a math manipulative to match anyone's fancy. This tried-and-true method uses a variety of materials—often recyclable objects—to

Manipulatives that are used well are central to effective instruction and have the capacity to greatly improve and deepen student understanding.

—Teaching and Learning Math

Most manipulatives can be used in many ways. Rather than use attribute blocks for classifying, students may choose a stack of them. For comparing and measuring piles, make one-dimensional designs (for exploring geometry and symmetry), count the pieces (for developing number senses and counting and calculating skills), or overlap shapes (for exploring part-whole relationships).

—Daniel Heuser

make math manipulatives. This method not only eases a teacher's financial burden but also teaches children to be stewards of our environment.

Still other books may lead to the use of commercially manufactured math manipulatives—colored cubes, dominoes, calculators, attribute blocks, abacus, sorting materials, and more.

Apply the following table to reinforce the literature and hands-on linkages while providing examples of the three categories of math manipulative materials: *Found Materials, Teacher/Student Prepared Materials,* and *Commercial Materials.* Through text and illustrations, the literature raises the idea of relevant materials for effective math investigations.

Literature and Math Manipulative Connections

Category	Concrete Manipulative	Literature	Strand	Virtual Manipulative
Found Materials	marbles, jellybeans, buttons, dried beans, shells	*Great Estimations* Bruce Goldstone	Number Sense and Numeration	
Teacher/ Student- Prepared	materials to create opportunities (e.g., card games, songs) to reinforce the concept	*Lots and Lots of Zebra Stripes* Stephen Swinburne	Patterning and Algebra	*Color Patterns Pattern Blocks*
Commercial	variety of Geometric solids (e.g., wood, foam, plastic)	*3-D Figures!* Kari Gold	Geometry and Spatial Sense	*Geoboard-Isometric*

Found Materials

Found materials are plentiful and easily accessible. Developing concepts of estimation is no small feat.

Great Estimations

The notion of estimating or knowing whether one's answer is "in the zone," should be introduced at an early age.

—Barry Onslow

Bruce Goldstone's *Great Estimations* presents techniques for guessing using collections (toys, buttons, seeds, beans), encouraging math awareness and quantity recognition through text and illustration. The beginning pages introduce the basic idea of making estimations, and then offer increasingly difficult examples to train the eye to remember. Goldstone uses a series of questions related to the illustrations. This book goes beyond requiring primary students to focus only on finding the number of items in a container to offering strategies for arriving at estimates that are close to the real number. Clearly, it invites children to make their own collections using found materials (e.g., marbles, jellybeans, buttons, shells). Children must have hands-on experiences with numbers if they are to understand them. *Great Estimations* can inspire students in making their own jar of objects they bring into the classroom to learn more about how to make estimates closer to the actual number of objects. The most common task is to have students estimate the number of objects in the jar and count them to find out the actual number.

Our role as teachers is to encourage our students to reflect on and use a variety of estimation strategies. We need to encourage our students to engage in estimation hands-on activities to help them develop a sense of number, size, and quantity.

Teacher/Student-Prepared Materials

Lots and Lots of Zebra Stripes

In *Lots and Lots of Zebra Stripes,* Stephen Swinburne sets the stage for thinking about patterns by focusing entirely on patterns and where they are found in nature. He defines patterns as "lines and shapes that repeat" and describes these patterns in both general and specific terms. For example, a grouping of clouds lasts "only a short time" and a spider's web is viewed as a series of spirals. Swinburne poses questions designed to help students think about their own environments. Students are inspired to look for patterns in likely places such as flowers and insects as well as in unlikely ones such as the inside of their lunch sack. This is an excellent introduction to pattern recognition and a wonderful way to demonstrate its real-world applications. *Lots and Lots of Zebra Stripes* could lead to exploring patterns using pattern blocks, or students and teachers could prepare materials for further hands-on explorations in patterning. Making card games or creating songs such as "There Was an Old Lady Who Swallowed a Fly" all serve to reinforce the concept. To represent their learning, encourage students to use words, tables, graphs, symbols, and diagrams to analyze patterns and functions.

Commercial Materials

3-D Figures

There is a wide variety of manufactured materials on the market. In *3-D Figures* Kari Gold introduces a variety of geometric solids through text and illustration. This big book lends itself well to a read-aloud strategy in which students engage first in reading the text and then in manipulating the materials. Gold ensures key vocabulary (e.g., *cone, cube, cylinder*) relevant to 3-D shapes is introduced and matched up to the appropriate brightly colored 3-D shapes. Illustrations challenge students to become more aware of the real-life applications of 3-D figures in our environment. Gold leads children into using appropriate hands-on math manipulatives to explore and investigate the properties of 3-D shapes. Make a wide variety of 3-D math manipulatives (wood, foam, plastic) accessible for all students in the classroom to strengthen their understanding of 3-D shapes. Extend their learning by making available 3-D Geometric Stamps and Folding Geometric Solids.

I have carefully chosen the math books recommended in *Math Memories You Can Count On* to represent these three methods of encouraging math manipulative usage in the primary classroom. We need to ensure children will have plenty of opportunities to explore, discover, and investigate in a hands-on learning environment. To illustrate how hands-on manipulatives can be used with text and illustrations in the classroom, I have provided below an example of one recommended title and its related math manipulative for each of the five strands.

Number Sense and Numeration

If a Chicken Stayed for Supper by Carrie Weston

When Mommy Fox goes hunting for a chicken for supper, her five cubs can't wait. They sneak out of their den and one of them gets lost. As the story unfolds, the five little foxes take turns counting one another until the mystery of the lost one is solved. Weston sets the stage for thinking about counting, beginning with a strong clue on the cover of this book. For example, illustrations of five bright little red foxes on the cover encourage very young children to count to five. Using this book can lead to developing an understanding of whole numbers, including concepts of correspondence, counting, cardinality, and comparison. Weston reinforces children's understanding of one-to-one correspondence through the text, graphics, and illustrations.

Mommy Fox is proud of the chicken soup she makes for supper. Weston includes drawings of the soup bowls to encourage children to use one-to-one correspondence to solve problems by matching sets. They compare number amounts and count objects to five and beyond.

Literature/Hands-on Extension

Prepare number word cards to five and make counting materials accessible for students. In partners, one student holds up a number word card while the other partner counts out the specific number of objects to match the number word. Students switch roles to allow the other partner a new opportunity to work with the numbers.

Measurement

Measuring Up by Jennifer Osborne

Even the cover of Osborne's big book draws young children's interest into the world of measurement. Realistic shots of measuring tapes spread out and over-lap to create this spectacular cover, reinforcing the hands-on math literature links. Throughout the book are unconventional measurement methods (measuring with our feet, our hands, paper clip chains) and conventional ones (rulers, measuring tapes). Osborne highlights related math vocabulary, emphasizing the place of literacy in mathematics. She goes beyond the measuring tape to include a wide variety of measurement tools. Clocks, thermometers, weigh scales, and a measuring cup are but a few. Osborne makes inquiry the centre-piece of learning. Beginning with a simple question, "How heavy is the food?" and progressing to a higher-level one, "How will they measure the sugar they need"? naturally prompts higher-level thinking in which students must compare and choose the appropriate measuring tool for the task. Finally, Osborne challenges children to look at the length of an object and guess which tool they would use to complete the task.

Literature/Hands-on Extension

Arrange children in groups of five. On each table, place five objects and a collection of measuring tools. Post a two-column chart with "yes" and "no" choices.

Have each student independently choose an object and decide what unit of measurement he or she would use to measure his or her object. When the task is complete, invite group members to discuss the choices and decide whether to make a check mark in the "yes" or "no" column. Allow time for each group to present their findings.

Geometry and Spatial Sense

Sir Cumference and the Sword in the Cone—A Math Adventure by Cindy Neuschwander

Sir Cumference, Radius, and Sir Vertex search for Edgecalibur, the sword King Arthur has hidden in a geometric solid. Charming text and illustrations combine to introduce children to geometric solids. Strong linkages between the Geometry and Spatial Sense strand in Mathematics and the Structures and Mechanisms Strand in Science evolve throughout the book, reinforcing meaningful understanding of the concepts and skills implicit in these two disciplines.

Literature/Hands-on Extension

The literature leads students to investigate 3-D solids and their relationships and applications. In linking literature, science, mathematics, and technology in appropriate contexts, children continue to develop their math concepts and skills while building a stronger understanding of interdisciplinary connections and reinforcing their literacy skills.

Algebra

Rooster's Off to See the World by Eric Carle

Understanding patterns and relationships begins in the Early Years. Students move from growing patterns and shrinking patterns generated by the repeated addition or subtraction of ones, twos, and fives on a number line and a hundreds chart to using a variety of tools (e.g., pattern blocks, attribute blocks) and drawings to demonstrate repeating patterns. There is no shortage of ideas to build students' algebraic thinking skills.

Patterns are embedded in familiar songs, poems, and stories. Using children's literature to integrate algebraic thinking provides an engaging forum for students to remember the story, song, or poem and its related investigation and remember the mathematics. Questions such as "How did you arrive at your pattern?" serve to facilitate the kind of classroom discourse that builds students' algebraic thinking skills.

Literature/Hands-on Extension

In small groups, students create pattern cards. They take turns to clap, snap, or stamp their feet to the patterns in the large group. Have them extend their work to create their own patterns using the pattern blocks.

Data Analysis

Tally O'Malley by Stuart J. Murphy

In *Tally O'Malley,* the math concept is tallying. Tally marks are a useful tool for children as they learn how to keep track of objects they are counting and data they collect over time. Grouping the tally marks also reinforces the ability to count by fives. Murphy tells his story of the O'Malley kids who begin counting all the gray cars or green T-shirts they see while on their way to a beach holiday. The long, boring drive motivates the three children to play tally games. The sample tally sheet embedded in the cover helps the reader know that this book will introduce the useful skill of tallying as a method of recording and displaying data collection.

Collecting and organizing data begins at an early age and continues throughout our lives. Found materials lend themselves nicely to collecting and organizing data. Strong linkages between the text and hands-on opportunities abound. This life skill begins with children collecting and organizing primary data based on qualities such as color. Children learn how to display the data using a variety of simple recording methods (arranging objects, placing stickers, drawing pictures, making tally marks). Throughout the primary grades, children progress from making simple bar graphs to other graphic organizers and display the data in charts, tables, and graphs. The last two pages of *Tally O'Malley* supply simple, practical, and doable ideas for teachers to extend student learning.

Literature/Hands-on Extension

Arrange children in small groups of four. Ask them to bring in a collection of found materials such as pebbles, marbles, and buttons; put a limit of 20 like objects. Make available a four-column chart tally sheet. To reinforce one-to-one correspondence in solving problems by matching sets, ask each student to count the number of objects in his/her collection and use a tally mark for each single object. Count the tally marks and indicate the total number of objects in each individual collection.

Reading stories that lead naturally to problem posing and having manipulatives accessible provides students the tools they need to work successfully toward solving problems kinesthetically. Teachers need to tap into students' varying learning styles in primary classrooms. Meeting the needs of some students may mean reading stories to help them understand ideas through context or visuals. For others, a technological experience such as using virtual manipulatives may be best.

Technology Link – Virtual Manipulatives

A Virtual Manipulative is "an interactive, Web-based visual representation of a dynamic object that presents opportunities for constructing mathematical knowledge."

— Moyer, Bolyard & Spikell

Using the computer mouse to control the physical actions of objects by sliding, flipping, turning, and rotating affords students opportunities to construct meaning on their own. Even if there are enough concrete materials to go around the class, teachers are encouraged to provide opportunities for students to experience using virtual manipulatives.

Benefits

- Allows for differentiated instruction.
- Helps students to see and explore difficult math concepts.
- Provides instant feedback.

The National Library of Virtual Manipulatives makes available the virtual manipulatives related to each strand. It groups the manipulatives by grade level for use in conjunction with the literature.

Five Easy Steps for Using Manipulatives in the Primary Classroom

Although the task may seem overwhelming, organizing your classroom to link children's literature effectively with hands-on manipulatives can be handled simply. Consider using a mathematics learning cart with sufficient space to store the literature and manipulatives. In one physical space, the two elements of an effective mathematics program are easily linked together.

1. Make manipulatives accessible for all students.
2. Set guidelines for their use.
3. Allow students explore time.
4. Ask questions/pose challenges.
5. Use appropriate assessment strategies to check for understanding.

Literature and Math Manipulative charts are good organizational tools. They link specific literature and manipulatives to provide a handy guide to some of the resources readily available for the math/literature connection.

As Greg Tang states in his book *MATH-terpieces*, "When given a choice of how to solve a problem children gravitate toward math manipulatives because they can act out the situations or relationships in the problem."

6 Investigating Appropriate Methods to Measure Growth in Math Understanding

Assessment and Evaluation Strategies

Assessment Provides Data

Assessment is the process of continuously gathering information about student learning and performance using a variety of sources—for example, projects—that accurately reflects how well a student is achieving the learning expectations.

Evaluation Brings Meaning

Evaluation refers to the process of judging the quality of student work, with assessments based on established criteria—as in rubrics—and assigning a value to represent the quality of how each criterion was met.

By doing ongoing, non-structured observations we assess students in context.

—Stenmark & Bush

The purpose of assessment has shifted from holding students accountable for learning to engaging student involvement in assessment to improve student learning. Assessment can be used to help students build confidence, motivate them to believe in themselves as capable learners, and serve as a strong foundation for important achievement gains for them.

—Rick Stiggins

Assessment and evaluation address both the processes and products of student work. How students work is the process, and the products that children produce are things such as surveys, games, scale drawings, and models. Assessment is a continuous process involving listening, observing, and asking questions to promote intellectual growth.

Effective mathematics assessment is ongoing and promotes continual growth in students' mathematics learning over time.

Assessment guides instruction, and instruction guides assessment. Teachers are encouraged to match the assessment techniques with the style of instruction and learning. New methods of assessment allow teachers to evaluate children's conceptual development and their process skills and problem-solving abilities.

Implementing a good mathematics program requires the use of a broad range of assessment techniques. *Math Memories You Can Count On* integrates many assessment techniques with the suggested hands-on interactive tasks that lead students to discover, construct, investigate, predict, represent, and engage in other math-related actions. Through these assessment techniques, teachers become familiar with their strengths, efficiencies, and appropriateness. Selecting the assessment technique that works best for a particular situation becomes an easier task.

Teachers must be aware of, and adapt to, the broad range of students in a class. It's possible that as many as half the students in a single class will require program modifications. Research about students' learning styles and multiple kinds of intelligence indicates that no *one* form of assessment can possibly fit each individual student's needs, because every student learns and performs differently—even from one time to the next.

In a mathematics program, it is critical to develop tasks that assess the mathematical ideas children are learning, and the children's conceptual understanding and ability to use mathematics skills and processes. "How can I assess the children's use of math manipulatives?" is a common question asked by teachers who are planning their math program. The use of hands-on math manipulatives allows for a more varied approach to assessment. The key is to assess students' knowledge, skills, and concepts in a variety of different situations using a variety of assessment strategies. Observation, conferences, interviews, performance tasks, and more allow teachers to observe and record students' actions and responses while they are working on math tasks.

Choosing which assessment strategy to use can, however, be difficult without guidelines.

This chapter will assist you in ensuring a balance among the assessment strategies available within a math hands-on problem-solving environment. *Math*

Memories You Can Count On suggests teachers share with students the purpose of the task, the method, and how the assignment/task is to be evaluated *prior to engaging students in the task.* By identifying the Big Ideas for each unit ahead of time, teachers can work back in order to plan their teaching. Preplanning the assessment activities and techniques teachers will use with students will also help ensure adequate demonstration of their learning.

The focus is always on what the student has achieved in relation to the Big Ideas… and on how that achievement has been demonstrated.

Assessment – Processes and Products

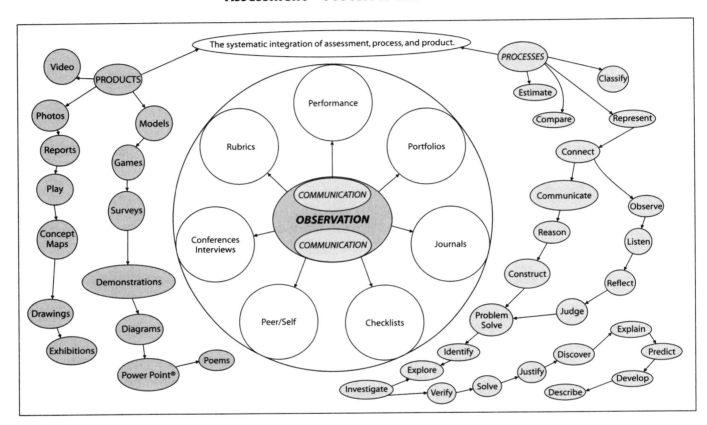

Excellence in classroom assessment will come when we can balance a number of assessment strategies and use them to help students learn (assessment for learning). At the same time, we need to use some assessments to verify that students did meet academic achievement standards (assessment of learning).

— Rick Stiggins

The next step is identifying an instructional approach to ensure learning opportunities for all students. With a diverse group of students, the literature-based approach to teaching math can be extremely useful. Literature serves as a catalyst for posing questions. Questions naturally emerge from the text and illustrations within each book. Hands-on math activities developed from the literature provide children with experience in using relevant math manipulatives for developing a foundation for learning concepts that are more abstract. For example, students can learn about geometry using a wide variety of 2- and 3-D manipulatives. Students with different learning styles, or aspects of multiple intelligences, can grasp the same mathematical concepts when they are introduced in trade books that match their learning patterns and areas of interest.

By combining the literature, hands-on math manipulatives, and a variety of student-centred assessment techniques—such as journals, portfolios, peer and self-evaluation, and interviews—teachers can ensure that all students have the opportunity to succeed.

Methods for Gathering Assessment Information

Observation

Observation is a systematic process of observing and recording student behavior that indicates the extent to which students understand concepts. Teachers can employ anecdotal notes, checklists, photos, and so on to document the observations made.

Teachers must be skilled in using observation data as an entrée into exploring the mathematics potential of books.

PURPOSE

- Allow for observing and recording how students approach learning tasks.
- Ensure listening to students ideas.
- Ask questions that probe students' thinking.

USE

- Provide systematic, ongoing information about students.
- Provide a forum for student feedback.
- Data can be used for conducting parent interviews.
- Data can be collected and used to help in determining grades.

ADVANTAGES

- Provide information about students, for example: attitudes, learning styles, ability to use math language and concepts

LINKING MATH AND ASSESSMENT

Observation is a useful means for identifying student progress in mathematics. The challenge is to make it a meaningful and purposeful strategy to monitor student progress. For example, if we want to observe how students sort and classify objects in a number of situations, we can observe using a checklist that outlines the specific criteria to focus on, for example, flexibility in approaches, broad or narrow categories, and related language. Checklists and anecdotal notes are two methods of recording ongoing observations. If we are observing how students sort and classify objects in a number of situations, we may want to preplan a number of questions.

IMPLEMENTING OBSERVATION IN THE PRIMARY CLASSROOM

Knowing what to observe is critical to gathering authentic data that lead to meaningful and purposeful learning. When math subtasks are based on established criteria, it's easy to observe how students manipulate relevant concrete math materials to demonstrate their learning. Observing how students complete the subtasks can provide insight into the next steps to move students forward in their math learning. Taking notes to help with planning individual and whole-class instruction is an important step.

Performance Assessment

Performance assessment occurs when a student conducts a task that enables teachers to see what that student knows about a specific topic. Through the tasks, teachers can more easily assess what students know and can do.

- Note the concepts and skills you expect students to know, to do, and to apply.
- Select assessment techniques that incorporate your students' learning styles.
- Choose assessment techniques that directly relate to the tasks.

The Role of the Student

- Monitor progress.
- Reflect on learning.
- Evaluate understanding

Performance assessment allows students to demonstrate their knowledge, skills, and the concepts they have gained through working with the Big Ideas.

PURPOSE

- Encourage learners to demonstrate knowledge, skills, and attitudes.
- Allow for the evaluation of practical skills and application of techniques.
- Allow for the evaluation of both process and product.
- Address all types of student evaluation—diagnostic, formative, and summative.

USE

- Begin where the students are.
- Effective in assessing process skills and problem-solving abilities.
- Provide teachers with information about how the student understands and applies knowledge.

ADVANTAGES

- Enable students to rise to their highest performance levels.
- Encourage ongoing feedback.
- Enhance communication (visual, oral, written).
- Portray a real-life connection.
- Allow students to formulate their own ideas and questions.
- Accommodate special-needs students through an alternative assessment method.
- Require students to apply their knowledge and skills in context.

LINKING MATH AND ASSESSMENT

Performance assessment provides the means for evaluating the mathematical processes and the skills related to the Big Idea. The performance assessment technique provides children with the opportunity to demonstrate their understandings relating to the Big Ideas.

IMPLEMENTING PERFORMANCE ASSESSMENT IN THE PRIMARY CLASSROOM

Performance assessment strategies have great opportunities for application in the classroom. The first step in implementing this strategy is for teachers to determine what is to be assessed. This strategy goes hand in hand with observation. When students are demonstrating a task, teachers are observing according to a set of pre-established criteria. For example, if we want to see if students have established one-to-one correspondence per the Number Sense and Numeration strand, we might provide them with ten objects and observe them taking turns to count them out.

Peer and Self-Assessment/Checklists

Peer and self-assessment play a significant role in the learning process in any math classroom. For example, when students are required to select materials to include in their mathematics portfolios, they naturally reflect on their own learning. This act of reflection is an integral component of self-assessment. Self-assessment is an essential component of formative assessment. Students become confident, successful learners when they are deeply involved in ongoing self-assessment, in keeping records of their own growth, and in communicating with others about their own growth. (Stiggins, Rick. *An Introduction to Student-Involved Assessment for Learning.*) On the other hand, peer assessment occurs when other students in the class evaluate a students' work. Often, these strategies are already at work in the primary mathematics classroom. Students are afforded multiple opportunities to practice peer and self-assessment strategies. A variety of checklists are available to help students gain facility applying this double-sided strategy. Some schools set up math buddies so that students can routinely solve problems and share their problem-solving solutions.

PURPOSE

- Encourage students to take on more responsibility for their learning.
- Encourage students to become increasingly aware of their strengths, weaknesses, and attitudes.
- Encourage students to provide useful feedback to the other person.
- Enhance self-esteem.

USE

- Provide opportunities for students to assess themselves and others.
- Promote both peer and self-assessment as an ongoing part of a balanced assessment program.
- Provide a record of how students perceive their learning.

ADVANTAGES

- Students learn to take risks.
- Students grow to understand their own attitudes, skills, and knowledge.
- Students are engaged in developing their own learning criteria.
- Students are encouraged to take on more responsibility for their own learning.

LINKING MATH AND ASSESSMENT

Students can assess themselves and others only when they have a clear picture of the target expectations for their learning. Teachers need to share the learning of the Big Ideas with their students. It is important to set aside a large time block so that students can question and discuss anything they need to find out about. Provide checklists of indicators/descriptors that you and your students should use for a given task. These provide a sense of direction. Checklists can also serve as a guide for students when assessing their own work and the work of others.

IMPLEMENTING PEER AND SELF-ASSESSMENT IN THE PRIMARY CLASSROOM

The role of the teacher in establishing peer and self-assessment in is to develop student skills in assessing and connecting their own work according to the expectations. It is truly rewarding for both students and the teacher when students feel comfortable enough to incorporate peer and self-assessment strategies. For this strategy to be effective, students must have the necessary skills, and teachers should teach these to students if they are not already familiar with them.

Conference/Interview

Insight into students' thinking is revealed by listening to their talk. Conversations with students can help us understand what they know and how they think.

— *A Guide to Effective Instruction in Mathematics, Kindergarten to Grade 3*

The interview and conference are two assessment strategies that are gaining momentum in mathematics classrooms. Although conducting an interview requires a substantial amount of time, there is a place for it in our classrooms. When trying to determine the difficulties a student is having with a particular concept or skill, teachers ask a question or series of questions to determine the student's depth of understanding.

Conferences provide a forum for students to talk about what they have learned. Teachers gather information about a student's progress and determine next steps. It's wise to plan questions ahead of time to stay focused on what you hope to get out of the conversation with your student. Questions such as "What would you like to understand more about?" "Is there another way to solve this problem?" help guide the conversation. Be sure to plan a reasonable block of time in which there won't be any interruptions. Always conclude with a summary sheet.

PURPOSE

- Provide an opportunity for students to "talk math."

USE

- Help identify student growth in mathematics over time.

ADVANTAGES

- More than talk.
- Allow time for individual discussions.
- Explore strengths and weaknesses, likes and dislikes.
- Empower students to take responsibility for part of the assessment of their own progress.
- Inform and motivate both student and teacher.
- Promote both student learning and their ability to use what they know.

LINKING MATH AND ASSESSMENT

Using a conference or interview strategy to gather key information on a student's attitude toward mathematics, the processes used, and products, provides key information for teachers to uncover barriers to mathematical understandings. Devising specific questions ahead of time in all three areas (attitudes, processes, and products) will help keep the discussion going in the right direction.

IMPLEMENTING CONFERENCES/INTERVIEWS IN THE PRIMARY CLASSROOM

In preparation for the interview/conference, ask students to bring a piece of work, a portfolio, or a visual representation to the conference as evidence to support the topic of conversation. Prepare questions ahead of time that target the topic. Plan for a block of uninterrupted time to conduct the interview/conference. Remember to take notes to reflect on at a future date to aid in planning effective lessons that move the student forward.

Rubrics

A rubric allows not only teachers and students but also parents/guardians to be partners in the assessment process. This assessment technique describes the criteria by which a student product, performance, or demonstration will be assessed. It serves a dual purpose: When properly constructed, it can guide and improve instruction while also serving as an assessment strategy. Rubrics outline and define levels of achievement and quality of work related to a specific task or set of tasks. The success of the rubric rests on how clearly it communicates the expected criteria for achievement to both students and parents.

PURPOSE

- Define standards for students and parents.
- Provide clear criteria on achievement for students.
- Promote and improve student self-assessment.
- Assist students in understanding the learning expectations and how they might improve the quality of their work.

USE

- Provide students with a clear idea of what they are doing well, what they need to work at more, and the next steps for improving.
- Help enhance student performance by defining the criteria of specific achievement.

ADVANTAGES

- Reveal a strong, high-quality assessment process.
- Allow students to see what went well and what didn't.
- Incorporate score sheets that spell out how a project, performance, or response will be marked.
- Encourage collaboration between and among colleagues of the same grade level.
- Provide teachers with a strong assessment tool for discussing with parents/guardians the basis of the grades they assign students.
- Improve student learning.
- Involve students in the assessment process.
- Make assessing student work quick and efficient.

LINKING MATH AND ASSESSMENT

Teachers of elementary mathematics have waited a long time for an assessment strategy they can apply in math teaching and learning to serve both instructional and assessment needs. The rubric is an authentic approach that fulfills this need. Students are eager to know how well they are doing and how they can improve their learning. Using a rubric as a means to evaluate mathematics teaching and learning—for example, criteria to identify how effectively math manipulatives are used—helps to improve our students' understanding of mathematics. Teachers are encouraged to use the four levels of achievement as points of reference in reviewing and determining how well students are achieving the expectations set for a specific area of study. The levels of achievement also provide students clear, authentic guidelines when they receive feedback on how well they have learned the knowledge, skills, and concepts set out in the rubric criteria.

Using this information provides them ongoing opportunities to improve their learning.

The preplanning stage is important in implementing rubrics as an assessment technique. Crucial to success is communicating a clear message to students and parents alike. Many teachers, children, and parents/guardians find it useful to discuss questions such as "What is a rubric?" "How will it be used?" "What place does it have in the math program?" Students want to know how they can become full partners in the learning process. When the true purpose is shared with students, they feel at ease and become better contributors in the development and implementation of rubrics in the mathematics classroom. Parents, too, are interested in knowing how their child will be evaluated. Taking time in the initial stages of implementation to explain these things to students and their parents/guardians is well worth the effort.

Recently I had the pleasure of observing a group of Grade 2 students work with their teacher to develop an assessment rubric. Their culminating task for a unit on weather was to make a model of a weather instrument to demonstrate their learning. The teacher led a discussion to establish a common understanding of how the models would be assessed. This resulted in the teacher/student co-development of a rubric. Students provided input around the criteria, and the teacher discussed the varying levels of achievement by which each model would be assessed. All students and parents had a copy of the rubric prior to the students' creations. By implementing this process, the assignment of grades is not a secret.

Portfolios

The portfolio contains a purposeful collection of samples of each student's work that shows progress, improvement, and significant learning. The portfolio should include items that the student feels represent his/her best work. The portfolio consists of student products that may include things like drawings, projects, photographs, or diagrams. The teacher and students work together to devise a method for storing the work samples, such as a homemade folder, box, album, or binder. Teachers can create a form for students to fill out and place in their storage container when videotapes or other such media devices or models are the means used to demonstrate student learning.

E-portfolios, digital collections of selected student work, are gaining momentum as an effective assessment strategy. Their ease of use encourages student, teacher, and parent sharing, reinforces technology skills, and demonstrates student learning throughout the year.

Digitally capturing students' growth throughout the year provides opportunities to assess learning and a whole lot more.

—Garthwait & Verrill

PURPOSE

- Provide ongoing records of student performance.
- Help students develop techniques such as self-evaluation in assessing their own work.
- Monitor growth of student knowledge, skills, and attitudes.
- Allow the student to express his/her learning in a variety of ways.

USE

- Monitor student progress.

- Teach children to reflect on what they have learned.
- Set goals for future improvement.

- Include concrete examples of student work.
- Provide opportunities for student/teacher/parent conferences.
- Allow for students with different learning styles.
- Show evidence of student self-reflection.
- Provide significant evidence of student progress.
- Allow students to be central to the process.
- Encourage active, self-directed learning.
- Provide opportunities for students to take ownership of their work.
- Offer a long-term record of student achievement.
- Encourage individual and group collaboration.
- Involve students in continuous assessment.
- Encourage effective written and oral communication.

LINKING MATH AND ASSESSMENT

Evaluation of portfolios varies according to the objectives of assignments. Many elementary teachers have found innovative ways to evaluate children's progress by using the portfolio.

Students who don't have the facility to read and write well can opt to put their collection in the portfolio as part of their overall assessment. What we must remember when using the portfolio for assessment, however, is to identify carefully the material that shows evidence of process, product, and interaction.

IMPLEMENTING PORTFOLIOS IN THE PRIMARY CLASSROOM

The organizational work behind implementing portfolios as an assessment strategy in primary classrooms needs to be in place before introducing the concept to students. The teacher needs to address questions such as "What should I expect students to include in the portfolio?" "How will I use it?" "How and where I will store it?" as part of the preplanning process.

Math Journals

The math journal provides students with the opportunity to express their thoughts, ideas, drawings, and even questions all in one place. Students write statements in their journals that address what they learned, what they do not understand, and what else they would like to know. Their journals may include key issues and concerns. It can be as simple as a student notebook, take on an elaborate shape, or be as topic-specific as you would like it to be.

PURPOSE

- Provide the opportunity for children to demonstrate their math and technology learning.
- Offer an avenue for students to reflect on their learning.
- Provide an opportunity for students to use math language when communicating.

- Provide a log for describing mathematical problems, procedures, observations, and solutions.
- Record students' growth in thinking and reflecting, and their conceptual understandings and attitudes.

ADVANTAGES

- Provide an opportunity to assess ongoing changes in children's understandings and thinking.
- Identify misconceptions.
- Provide proof of student learning and growth for parent/teacher conferences.
- Contain a record of students' observations, data, solutions to problems, drawings, written notes, questions, and so forth.

LINKING MATH AND ASSESSMENT

Teachers can assess math journals on a formal and/or informal basis. Assessment should be based on the criteria you and the children set. Use a rubric to effectively assess student journals and look for indicators of students' understanding, their level of interest in a topic, or their comprehension of related skills.

Educators continue to find innovative ways to evaluate children's progress using the math journal. This can be done quite simply by providing a context for children's journal entries.

IMPLEMENTING MATH JOURNALS IN THE PRIMARY CLASSROOM

Students may keep math journals for each of the topics they study during the year. Introduce the concept of the math journal to the children by sharing some books, such as *The Spider's Diary* and *Amelia's Notebook,* that illustrate the passage of time. Discuss the value of keeping a record of events to reflect on later. Discuss the components of a math journal: data gathered during an activity, drawings that illustrate a concept, and/or a story that describes something they learned.

Work with children to set assessment criteria that include "habits of mind" as well as knowledge and understanding. List the indicators that demonstrate the makings of a good math journal and post on the classroom wall for children's reference. Encourage children to use their math journals and have them share their entries in a large-group setting. Use math journals regularly as one method of assessing children's knowledge, skills, and attitudes.

Math photo journals can be a very interesting extension to the usual written format. Students of all grades can benefit from this format. For example, I worked with a group of junior students who were engaged in making 3-D models to demonstrate their new math learning in the Geometry and Spatial Sense strand. Throughout the process, they took digital photos at various points to indicate the different stages of construction. Using the photos and written statements indicating their learning helped strengthen their knowledge and understanding of geometry skills and concepts. The photo journal also served as a record of their learning.

The Ultimate Goal of Assessment

Sound assessment really requires a photo album approach where we look at various sources of evidence from different types of assessments put together in a photo album.

—Wiggins & McTighe

Using a variety of assessment strategies, we can help all students to succeed in communicating their knowledge of math content and math processes both within school and in the world outside of school.

In *Math Memories You Can Count On,* I have provided numerous opportunities for children to do math and use children's literature and math manipulatives throughout the five math strands developed in Chapter 7. Teachers can use innovative assessment strategies such as video quizzes, mini-plays based on conceptual development from the books, and rubrics for advertisements the children develop to promote their own assessment products. When we open ourselves to using new assessment strategies, we model the very habits of mind we want our students to demonstrate.

7   The Five Mathematics Strands

- Number Sense and Numeration
- Measurement
- Geometry and Spatial Sense
- Patterning and Algebra
- Data Management and Probability

Implementing the Literature-Based Approach in Teaching the Five Strands

Chapter 3: Building New Mathematics Memories details the benefits of using a literature-based approach to teaching the Mathematics strands. For more information on implementing the literature-based approach, see Chapter 4: Securing Long-Lasting Math Memories.

Each strand opens with an organizer identifying Sample Math-Related Manipulatives, the Big Ideas, and 15 Math-Related Literature Suggestions. Within each strand is a Classroom Implementation—Preplanning process chart. Included in the chart is an example of a related Big Idea and how the Big Idea is developed using the literature of the specific strand. A Big Idea Text Set, mathematics learning centres, assessment matrix, and a list of related literature are also included. There is a review of all 15 recommended books with a sample activity related to each book. Each strand concludes with a Literature/Math Manipulative Organizer.

The following checklist summarizes the seven easy steps for implementing the literature-based approach to teaching mathematics.

Getting Started – Seven Easy Steps

☑ 1. Select a Mathematics Strand and Big Idea.
☑ 2. Review the expectations related to the Big Idea.
☑ 3. Cluster the expectations around the Big Idea.
☑ 4. Choose an appropriate assessment strategy (or strategies).
☑ 5. Search for the related literature.
☑ 6. Think of a problem using the literature as a catalyst.
☑ 7. Choose an instructional approach (guided math, shared math, independent math).

Sample Math-Related Manipulatives

Number Sense and Numeration

BIG IDEAS

Operational Sense

Counting

Quantity

Relationships

Representation

Math-Related Literature Suggestions

Benny's Pennies Pat Brisson	**The Great Math Tattle Battle** Anne Bowen	**100th Day Worries** Margery Cuyler	**How Many Mice?** Michael Garland	**Numbers Every Day** Kari Gold
Subtraction Action Loreen Leedy	**Fraction Action** Loreen Leedy	**how many seeds in a pumpkin?** Margaret McNamara	**12 Ways to Get to 11** Eve Merriam	**Give Me Half** Stuart Murphy
Solve It Jennifer Osborne	**Count to a Million** Jerry Pallotta	**A Remainder of One** Elinor J. Pinczes	**The Grapes of Math** Greg Tang	**Math Potatoes** Greg Tang

Number Sense and Numeration

An understanding of place-value numeration occurs on many levels; it may include an understanding of tens and ones, computational procedures, decimal numerals, binary numerals, or scientific notation. Children in grades K–2 should use multiple models to develop initial understandings of place value and the base-ten system.

In grades 3–5, children should understand the place-value structure of the base-ten number system and be able to represent and compare whole numbers and decimals and recognize equivalent representations for the same number and generate them by decomposing and composing numbers.

— Sharon Ross

Mary's math memories have stayed with me for a great many years. While in a bookstore recently, I discovered *A Place for Zero: A Math Adventure* by Angeline LoPresti. This wonderful children's book emphasizes zero and its place-value role in our number system. I kept thinking about how valuable this book would have been for Mary's classmates and prospective teachers to help them make sense of the zero in the context of story.

Throughout this mathematical adventure, LoPresti plays with words as well as number concepts as she takes us into the land of Digitaria, ruled by King Multiplus and Queen Addeleine, where "every number knows its place." But Count Infinity, who formed the strange new digit Zero, doesn't know what to do with it, for it "meant nothing." Zero does work with the Count's Numberator machine, only to discover that adding himself doesn't change a number. But when he goes to the king and asks to be multiplied, fascinating results occur: more zeros and then combinations from ten on up.

Zero can be a more complicated concept than its "nothingness" suggests! Another excellent book for this purpose is Greg Tang's *The Best of Times*. Through poetry, Tang challenges children to acquire an intuitive understanding of the place of zero.

Children have difficulty learning place-value concepts. "Place-value, like many concepts, is often taught as though it were some sort of natural phenomenon... as if being in the 10s column was a simple, naturally occurring, observable property, like being tall or loud or round." (Garlikov, Richard. "The Concept and Teaching of Place-Value.") Using children's literature in the context of problem solving is an effective vehicle for promoting the understanding of place value, in which children understand place value to be about "how and why columns represent what they do and how they relate to each other, not just knowing what they are named." (Garlikov, Richard.) Linking literature to math manipulatives provides excellent opportunities for students to use a variety of appropriate manipulatives to deepen and extend their understanding of mathematical concepts. For example, you can project clear-view base-ten strips of tens and ones on an overhead projector to develop an interactive game that addresses place value, in which children tell how many they see. "Students who have used only base-ten materials to represent two-digit numbers may have a weaker conceptual understanding of place value than students who have also bundled craft sticks into tens and hundreds and used an abacus. (*The Ontario Curriculum: Mathematics*, 2005.)

Developing the Concept of Place Value

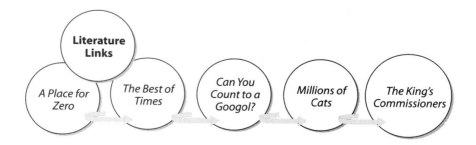

Many engaging children's books facilitate a deeper understanding of place value at various levels. A wonderful example is Robert Wells' *Can You Count to a Googol?* Wells introduces concepts of very large numbers, up to a googol, and multiples of ten. This resource develops understanding of place-value positions. Amazingly, *Millions of Cats* by Wanda Gag is as useful today as when it was published in 1928. It is one of the oldest picture books still in print, so it has to be good! Through story and illustrations, *Millions of Cats* invites children to develop foundation concepts of place value. The reader organizes millions of cats on a faraway hill in groupings of ones, tens, hundreds, and thousands… preparing him or her to apply rounding procedures and operating with larger numbers. One final recommendation I'd like to make is Aileen Friedman's *The King's Commissioners.* As children investigate the different methods employed by the royal advisors, this enchanting narrative stimulates discussion of place value concepts and calculation strategies. Friedman challenges the reader to think about the place value structure of our number system.

Research speaks to significant gains in conceptual understanding of place value when the learning of multi-digit concepts and procedures are treated as a conceptual problem-solving activity rather than as the transmission of rules and procedures. (Kamii, 1984.) The concept of number is often difficult to understand. It's important for students to learn how to work with numbers to develop number sense. "Computational fluency and number sense are intimately related. They develop together." (Sztajn, Paola. Dec. 2002. "Celebrating 100 with Number Sense." *Teaching Children Mathematics.*) Base-ten blocks are a great way to teach place value visually.

The Number Sense and Numeration strand addresses more than place value, however. Understanding and applying number and operations, representing numbers and relationships among numbers, counting, learning the basic operations, and problem-solving strategies form the centrepiece of this strand.

Classroom Implementation – Preplanning

STRAND: Number Sense and Numeration
BIG IDEA: Counting
KEY CONCEPTS/SKILLS: Ordering, one-to-one correspondence, cardinality, counting on, counting back
ASSESSMENT STRATEGY: Per Assessment Chart
TEXT SET: Select *relevant* Big Idea Text Set.

Understanding place value is important to achieving good number sense, estimating and using mental mathematics skills, and understanding multi-digit operations.

— *Teaching Children Mathematics*

We need to create opportunities or problems for children to explore, allow them to devise their own strategies and interact with them as they think or work through situations.

—Ann Anderson

Big Idea Text Set – Linking Math Manipulatives and Math-Related Literature

Counting

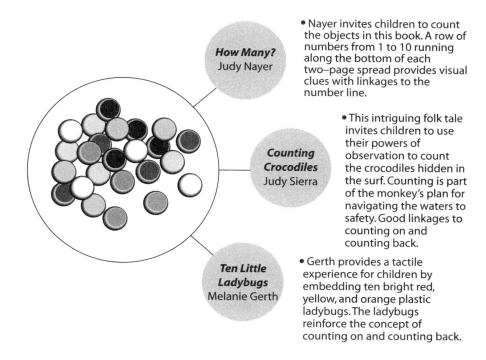

How Many?
Judy Nayer

- Nayer invites children to count the objects in this book. A row of numbers from 1 to 10 running along the bottom of each two-page spread provides visual clues with linkages to the number line.

Counting Crocodiles
Judy Sierra

- This intriguing folk tale invites children to use their powers of observation to count the crocodiles hidden in the surf. Counting is part of the monkey's plan for navigating the waters to safety. Good linkages to counting on and counting back.

Ten Little Ladybugs
Melanie Gerth

- Gerth provides a tactile experience for children by embedding ten bright red, yellow, and orange plastic ladybugs. The ladybugs reinforce the concept of counting on and counting back.

Problem: Question related to the underpinning concepts in the selected text.
Instructional Approach: Independent Math—Math Discovery Hubs

Classroom Example in Action

LEAD BOOK: *How Many?*
READ AND DISCUSS: In a large group, read the big book *How Many?*
ENGAGE: Provide opportunities for students to engage in the text. For example, counting the objects aloud, repeating the number as a large group, selecting the matching number from a number line at the bottom of the two-page spread… and more.
POSE RELATED QUESTION: *What other ways are there to count?*

Number Sense and Numeration Discovery Hub

Counting

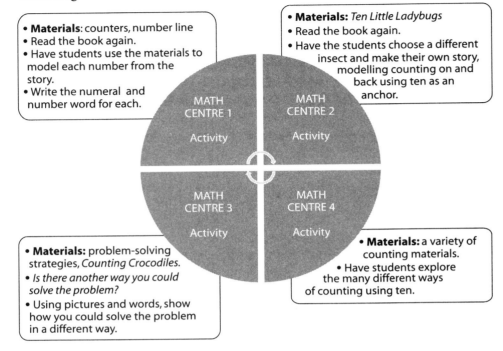

- **Materials**: counters, number line
- Read the book again.
- Have students use the materials to model each number from the story.
- Write the numeral and number word for each.

MATH CENTRE 1

Activity

- **Materials:** *Ten Little Ladybugs*
- Read the book again.
- Have the students choose a different insect and make their own story, modelling counting on and back using ten as an anchor.

MATH CENTRE 2

Activity

MATH CENTRE 3

Activity

- **Materials:** problem-solving strategies, *Counting Crocodiles.*
- *Is there another way you could solve the problem?*
- Using pictures and words, show how you could solve the problem in a different way.

MATH CENTRE 4

Activity

- **Materials:** a variety of counting materials.
- Have students explore the many different ways of counting using ten.

OTHER COUNTING BOOK SUGGESTIONS

Aker, Suzanne. *What Comes in 2s, 3s & 4s?*
Giganti, Paul. *Each Orange Had 8 Slices.*
McNamara, Margaret. *how many seeds in a pumpkin?*
Schlein, Miriam. *More Than One.*

Linking Math Centre Activities and Assessment Strategies

Activity	Observation	Interview/ Conference	Portfolio	Self/Peer	Performance	Math Journal	Rubric	Checklist
1	✔							
2							✔	
3					✔			
4		✔						

Recommended Books, Sample Activities, and a Suggested Process for Implementing the Number Sense and Numeration Strand

Benny's Pennies by Pat Brisson

SUMMARY: The main character, Benny McBride, has five new pennies to spend. Illustrations reveal how Benny could spend his money and encourage children to make their own predictions. This is a perfect read-aloud story with lots of possibilities for students to think, predict, and interact with the text. Tactile experiences abound. This book can be used as a springboard to introducing the nickel, dime, and quarter.

CONNECTING STRAND: Data Management and Probability

READ AND DISCUSS: *Benny's Pennies*

POSE RELATED QUESTION: *Can you think of a way you could show how Benny spent his money?*

SAMPLE ACTIVITY: Introduce the pictograph. With a large group of students, use money stamps to develop a cooperative coin graph based on the story. In small groups, have students choose three things they would buy if they had Benny's pennies and make a graph showing how the money was spent.

The Great Math Tattle Battle by Anne Bowen

SUMMARY: Harley Harrison is the best math student in the Grade 2 class and the biggest tattletale. He keeps track of his classmates' comings and goings, using his number sense to record such details as the number of erasers a student chews. Harley totals up these infractions weekly, turning in a report to his teacher. Throughout the book, Bowen poses problems that require calculations using addition, subtraction, and multiplication. She provides a two-page spread of problems to solve at the back of the book (Math Tattle Battle Teasers). Bowen invites children to solve the problems the best way they know how.

CONNECTING STRAND: Data Management and Probability

READ AND DISCUSS: *The Great Math Tattle Battle*

POSE RELATED QUESTION: *What makes a good problem?*

SAMPLE ACTIVITY: Have each student make up a problem similar to the Math Tattle Battle Teasers. Create a class problem-solving big book. Challenge students to find their own ways to solve the problems. Have students place their problem-solving methods into a large envelope. Invite a few individual students to share their problem-solving methods on a regular basis.

100th Day Worries by Margery Cuyler

SUMMARY: *100th Day Worries* is the story of a girl who must bring a collection of one hundred things to school for the 100th day school celebration. Since she couldn't make up her mind on what to take to school, her family members gave her each groups of ten things to take. The book's illustrations, text, and symbols reflect a mathematician method. For example, mental calculation strategies, including skip counting, making tens, repeated addition, and building on a known sum of ten are used to count each student's collection.

CONNECTING STRAND: Data Management and Probability

READ AND DISCUSS: *100th Day Worries*. This is a good opportunity to investigate place value.

POSE RELATED QUESTION: *What would you choose to make up your own personal collection of 100 things?*

SAMPLE ACTIVITY: Have students bring in 100 items and organize them into groups of 10. Have them think of a way to represent their collections (e.g., pictograph, bar graph).

How Many Mice? by Michael Garland

SUMMARY: This is a tale of addition and subtraction. Ten hungry mice set off to gather food. Along the way, they encounter other animals who take their food. The mice have to make up the difference. Garland engages children throughout the text by posing questions such as "How many pieces of food do the mice have now?" Garland hides the questions in illustrations that challenge children to observe carefully.

CONNECTING STRAND: Data Management and Probability

READ AND DISCUSS: *How Many Mice?*

POSE RELATED QUESTION: *If each mouse eats two things, how many mice will it take to eat all the food?*

SAMPLE ACTIVITY: Encourage students to use the counting materials to discover an answer to the problem. Have students think of a way they can share their solution.

Numbers Every Day by Kari Gold

SUMMARY: Gold provides numerous examples of how numbers are used in real life (e.g., to measure, to buy, to cook, to find mass). Each large spread asks a different question. These questions require children to observe, predict, and compare. Gold introduces math-related language (e.g., *kilograms, first, second, pair, dozen*).

CONNECTING STRAND: Measurement

READ AND DISCUSS: *Numbers Every Day*

POSE RELATED QUESTION: *What other ways are numbers used in the schoolyard?*

SAMPLE ACTIVITY: Arrange students in small groups. Have them go on a number walk and challenge each group to find one way numbers are used in the schoolyard. Take along a digital camera and record each group's findings. Make a class photo display.

Subtraction Action by Loreen Leedy

SUMMARY: This book is set in the context of a school math fair. Leedy introduces children to mathematical concepts involving subtraction skills through the activities of animal students at the school fair. Children are given a helping hand in solving the problems. Cartoon illustrations and dialog balloons in each chapter supply the information children need to solve problems. Two- and three-digit equations, including money equations, are embedded in the text. Leedy provides math-related language throughout the book (e.g., *less, minus, difference*).

CONNECTING STRAND: Measurement

READ AND DISCUSS: *Subtraction Action*

POSE RELATED QUESTION: *What one clue would you provide for a friend who wanted to get better at solving problems?*

SAMPLE ACTIVITY: Have each small group create a problem requiring subtraction. Ask students to exchange their problem with another group and try to solve their problem. Have students discuss and share what strategies they used to solve their problem.

Fraction Action by Loreen Leedy

SUMMARY: Animal characters and enchanting illustrations help introduce the concept of fractions. The colorful story format helps children explore fractions by finding many examples in the world around them. Examples such as geometric shapes divided into sections make it easy for children to visualize what is meant by the various amounts. Dividing objects into equal parts and subtracting and comparing the value of fractions are two subject-related areas addressed in *Fraction Action*.

CONNECTING STRAND: Measurement

READ AND DISCUSS: *Fraction Action*

POSE RELATED QUESTION: *In what other ways are fractions used in the real world?*

SAMPLE ACTIVITY: Have students use manipulatives to represent fractions introduced in the book. Make available a variety of materials—from magnetic to foam and plastic —to explore fractions. Encourage students to divide whole objects into parts and identify and describe equal-sized parts of the whole, using fractional names (halves, fourths, quarters).

how many seeds in a pumpkin? by Margaret McNamara

SUMMARY: This book engages children in counting pumpkin seeds using three different-sized pumpkins. Throughout the text, children meet math concepts embedded in the

Big Idea: counting (ordinals, cardinality, estimation, skip counting). Children pose guesses and count the seeds from each pumpkin to find out which pumpkin has the most seeds. Everyone is amazed to discover that the smallest pumpkin has the most seeds. Two connecting math strands ensure numerous opportunities for students to engage in mathematics concepts and skills.

CONNECTING STRANDS: Measurement, Data Management and Probability

READ AND DISCUSS: *how many seeds in a pumpkin?*

POSE RELATED QUESTION: *Which pumpkin has the least number of seeds?*

SAMPLE ACTIVITY: Make available three jars with different quantities of jellybeans. Ask: *What jellybean jar has the least number of jellybeans in it?* Have students pose guesses and count the jellybeans in each jar to offer an accurate number. Invite students to make a bar graph representing their learning.

12 Ways to Get to 11 by Eve Merriam

SUMMARY: This charming counting book uses ordinary experiences to present the twelve number combinations that add up to eleven. Every two pages focus on a different way to get to the number eleven. Merriam introduces the concept "All whole number quantities are compositions of other smaller quantities."

CONNECTING STRAND: Patterning and Algebra

READ AND DISCUSS: *12 Ways to Get to 11*

POSE RELATED QUESTION: *What other combinations of numbers can you think of?*

SAMPLE ACTIVITY: Make counting materials accessible for students to try out different combinations of numbers. Have them work in small groups to come up with their own number stories. Ask students to write additional number sentences that identify the combinations of numbers that when added together equal a larger number.

Give Me Half by Stuart J. Murphy

SUMMARY: This rhyming story about a brother and sister who do not want to share their food introduces the concept of halves. It can act as a springboard to introduce dividing whole objects into halves and sets of objects into equal parts. Children understand how to divide whole objects into halves and identify and describe equal-sized parts of the whole using the fractional name. Murphy includes two pages of suggestions for engaging hands-on activities focusing on the understanding of halves. He includes experiences such as cooking, nature, and games that are fun while extending students' knowledge and understanding of halves. The book introduces new terms (for example, *divide)* and gives the reader an enjoyable introduction to fractions.

CONNECTING STRANDS: Patterning and Algebra, Geometry and Spatial Sense

READ AND DISCUSS: *Give Me Half*

POSE QUESTION: *How many equal-sized parts can you make using a variety of geometric shapes?*

SAMPLE ACTIVITY: Make accessible a variety of geometric shapes. Have students investigate equal-sized parts of the whole, using the fractional name (e.g., *halves).* Extend their learning to include fourths or quarters.

Solve It! by Jennifer Osborne

SUMMARY: Problem solving underpins mathematics understanding in all the math strands. What better book than Osborne's to motivate students to learn how to solve problems? Osborne includes a series of questions that stimulate higher-level thinking, focusing children's attention on the early use of effective problem-solving strategies. She suggests math-related vocabulary, for example, *How many, more, lot, few, less, guess* that supplies clues to understanding and solving problems. Large colorful images work hand in hand with the text.

CONNECTING STRAND: Data Management and Probability
READ AND DISCUSS: *Solve It!*
POSE RELATED QUESTION: *Can word clues help you solve a problem? How?*
SAMPLE ACTIVITY: Have students pose a word problem using word clues to help others solve problems. Make a word-clue problem-solving wall and display in the classroom.

Count to a Million by Jerry Pallotta

SUMMARY: This book is one of the best for teaching place value. Although at the upper end of the primary grades students are required to count to 1000, children are intrigued to find out what lies beyond. Pallotta encourages an inquiring mind and seeks to build a level of confidence in mathematics throughout the text. He begins, "If you can count to ten, you can count to one million." Using basic math grouping skills and a positive attitude, math can be fun.

CONNECTING STRAND: Patterning and Algebra
READ AND DISCUSS: *Count to a Million*
POSE RELATED QUESTION: *What other ways are there to explore one million?*
SAMPLE ACTIVITY: Have students investigate one million using a variety of base-ten materials.

A Remainder of One by Elinor J. Pinczes

SUMMARY: Here is a good introduction to the concept of division and a springboard to discussing equal groupings. Twenty-five ants are divided into rows of two, then three, then four… all resulting in a remainder of one, until five rows of five conclude the story happily. *A Remainder of One* applies numerical division to a practical problem and explains it in an entertaining way.

CONNECTING STRAND: Patterning and Algebra
READ AND DISCUSS: *A Remainder of One*
POSE RELATED QUESTION: *What other ways can you group numbers to 100?*
SAMPLE ACTIVITY: Make math manipulatives accessible to students. Have them use the concrete material to assemble each formation in the book. Allow time for students to work in small groups to create number puzzles for classmates to solve. Arrange oral sharing of one method.

The Grapes of Math by Greg Tang

SUMMARY: Greg Tang presents mental addition strategies through patterns and combinations of numbers in rhyming verses that accompany illustrations. Children are inspired to use their problem-solving and critical-thinking skills to find solutions to problems. Tang includes solutions to the puzzles and addition strategies at the back of the book (e.g., symmetries and number combinations, patterns).

CONNECTING STRANDS: all strands
READ AND DISCUSS: *The Grapes of Math*
POSE RELATED QUESTION: *What riddle and corresponding illustration can you create to model a strategy for solving a problem?*
SAMPLE ACTIVITY: Invite students to make a poster showing picture and words that tell how you would go about solving the problem.

Math Potatoes by Greg Tang

SUMMARY: This book provides a problem-solving approach to addition and subtraction. Tang challenges children to think deeply about numbers in groups. Rhymes and riddles help children develop their math and problem-solving skills. Hidden in the riddles are problems. Tang poses a problem and offers clues to help children find smart ways to group numbers. The last few pages are saved for solutions, so children can see just how smart they were in solving problems successfully.

CONNECTING STRANDS: all strands

READ AND DISCUSS: *Math Potatoes*

POSE RELATED QUESTION: *What problem can you create?*

SAMPLE ACTIVITY: In small groups, have students create a different math problem. Rotate the problems around the classroom and have each group suggest a problem-solving strategy. Return the solution to the creators of the problem. Have each group read their problem aloud and encourage others to try to guess the appropriate problem-solving strategy.

Number Sense and Numeration – Literature/Math Manipulative Organizer

MATHEMATICAL PROCESSES

Problem Solving; Reasoning and Proving; Reflecting; Selecting Tools and Computational Strategies; Connecting; Representing; Communicating

Title/Author	Concepts/Skills/Topics/Additional Comments	Literary Style/Type	Math Manipulatives/Found Materials
Benny's Pennies Pat Brisson	Counting, money, ordering, number and operations, predicting	Fiction–rhyming text	Coin sets, money stamps
The Great Math Tattle Battle Anne Bowen	Addition, subtraction, multiplication, problem solving	Fiction–picture book	Problem-solving tools
100th Day Worries Margery Cuyler	Counting–skip counting	Fiction–story	Base-10 materials
How Many Mice? Michael Garland	Counting, addition, subtraction, operational sense	Fiction–story	Concrete materials, drawings, counters, number lines
Numbers Every Day Kari Gold	Real-world applications, number sense	Big book (read-aloud)–math concept book	Weigh scale, clocks
Subtraction Action Loreen Leedy	Subtraction, 3-digit equations, money, regrouping, problem solving	Fiction–story, concept book	Concrete materials, number line, pictures, drawings
Fraction Action Loreen Leedy	Fractions, problem solving–real-world applications	Fiction–story, concept book	Fraction kit
how many seeds in a pumpkin? Margaret McNamara	Skip counting, even/odd – 1s, 2s, 5s, 10s, estimating, ordinals, cardinality, guessing	Fiction–story	Weigh scale, graphing, counters
12 Ways to Get to 11 Eve Merriam	Addition, subtraction, counting, 12 groupings of numbers that add up to 12, number operations, number sense	Concept book	Counters
Give Me Half Stuart J. Murphy	Fractions, halves, whole, groups	Rhyming text–story	Fraction kit
Solve It! Jennifer Osborne	Problem-solving focus, read-aloud	Big book (read-aloud)–concept book	Tools for problem solving
Count to a Million Jerry Pallotta	Large numbers, counting	Concept book	Base-10 kit
A Remainder of One Elinor J. Pinczes	Division, problem solving	Fiction–verse and rhyme	Concrete materials
The Grapes of Math Greg Tang	Creative thinking, problem solving, riddles	Rhyming text	Tools for problem solving
Math Potatoes Greg Tang	Creativity, problem solving, groupings, finding patterns and symmetries, repeating groups, equal-sized groups	Rhyming text–poems and picture combination	Tools for problem solving

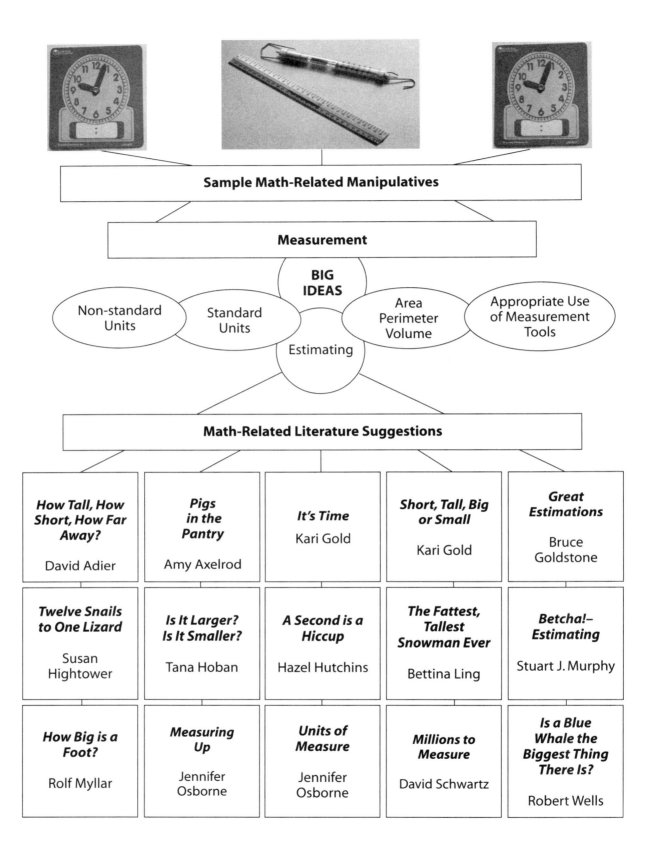

Sample Math-Related Manipulatives

Measurement

BIG IDEAS

Non-standard Units

Standard Units

Estimating

Area Perimeter Volume

Appropriate Use of Measurement Tools

Math-Related Literature Suggestions

How Tall, How Short, How Far Away? David Adier	***Pigs in the Pantry*** Amy Axelrod	***It's Time*** Kari Gold	***Short, Tall, Big or Small*** Kari Gold	***Great Estimations*** Bruce Goldstone
Twelve Snails to One Lizard Susan Hightower	***Is It Larger? Is It Smaller?*** Tana Hoban	***A Second is a Hiccup*** Hazel Hutchins	***The Fattest, Tallest Snowman Ever*** Bettina Ling	***Betcha!– Estimating*** Stuart J. Murphy
How Big is a Foot? Rolf Myllar	***Measuring Up*** Jennifer Osborne	***Units of Measure*** Jennifer Osborne	***Millions to Measure*** David Schwartz	***Is a Blue Whale the Biggest Thing There Is?*** Robert Wells

Measurement

The Measurement strand focuses on the Big Ideas of attributes, units of measurement, measurement sense, and measurement relationships to include non-standard units and standard units, comparing objects using measurable attributes, and investigating relationships. Many opportunities and experiences reflect more than one of the Big Ideas. Measurement is embedded across all strands, including number and geometry, and has numerous interdisciplinary connections. Instruction should progress through four stages in learning in each area of measurement:

- Make comparisons between objects by matching.
- Compare objects with non-standard units.
- Compare objects with standard units.
- Choose suitable units for specific measurements.

The mathematical processes—problem solving, reasoning and proving, reflecting, selecting tools and computational strategies, connecting, representing and communicating—are integrated throughout.

In the primary grades, students progress from identifying objects as "same" or "different," "more" or "less" based on attributes they can measure. Sharing such read-aloud big books as *More or Less?* by Judy Nayer and *Units of Measure* by Jennifer Osborne offers a context to introduce the language of measurement. The vocabulary is incorporated in the text and works with illustrations to help children identify measurable attributes such as length, weight, volume, area, and time. These attributes are introduced in the Early Years through play. Children begin to build their measurement sense, making direct comparisons of objects based on these attributes. It's important that manipulatives for measuring be accessible to provide the concrete experiences that assist children in understanding measurement to solve problems.

Quality children's literature supports students in their understanding of measurement. *Measuring Up* helps introduce children to non-standard units of measurement and makes them aware of standard units. Non-standard units make it easier to focus on the attribute being measured. Books such as *The Fattest Tallest Snowman Ever* and *How Big Is a Foot?* invite the use of non-standard units for beginning measurement activities for all primary students. The text and illustrations demonstrate the use of both non-standard concrete measuring objects (such as paper clips, hands, feet) and standard-unit measuring tools (such as rulers, measuring tapes, clocks, scales, measuring cups, thermometers).

Other concepts such as measuring perimeter, area, mass, capacity, and time, as well as estimating, can also be introduced through children's literature. I have recommended many books for this purpose in *Math Memories You Can Count On*. Big books such as Osborne's *Give It a Guess!* provide an opportunity for students to gain awareness of the size of different units and familiarity with the measuring process while engaged in estimating. *It's Time* by Kari Gold is a useful resource when addressing time.

The need to know and understand measurement is an important life skill. Measurement is all around us. Limitations not understood at first by younger children grow as they grow. I'm reminded of a time when I went to the fair grounds. I took a quick walk through the adult rides and noticed children had to be a certain height to go on some of the larger, more dangerous rides. To ensure safety measures were in place at all times, children were asked to measure them-

The world is filled with references to measurements that limit children's activities.

—Ashbrook, Peggy. *Science & Children*

selves against a black line that indicated whether they were big enough to ride on certain rides.

Classroom Implementation – Preplanning

STRAND: Measurement
BIG IDEA: Non-standard Units
KEY CONCEPTS/SKILLS: Understand attributes (e.g., length), select appropriate type of unit for measuring each attribute, become familiar with standard units in metric systems, comparing, estimating, judging, choosing
ASSESSMENT STRATEGY: Per Assessment Chart
TEXT SET: Create *relevant* Big Idea Text Set

Big Idea Text Set – Linking Math Manipulatives and Math-Related Literature

Non-standard Units

Measuring Up
Jennifer Osborne

- Measuring tapes adorn the cover of this big book, setting an early context. This concept book begins with non–standard units (e.g., feet, hand-to-hand) and progresses to standard units, introducing a variety of measurement tools—clock, thermometer, measuring tape, and cup. Children are challenged to make choices in selecting the right tool to suit its purpose. For example, "Which tool would you use to measure the length of a dog from nose to tail?"

How Big Is a Foot?
Rolf Myllar

- No one in the Kingdom knows the answer to this question: The king wishes to give the queen a special bed for her birthday and measures the size using his own foot. He gives the measurements to the carpenter, who gives them to the little apprentice. When the little apprentice builds the bed, he uses his own feet as a standard, and the bed is too small. How can they figure out what size the bed should be?

Is a Blue Whale the Biggest Thing There Is?
Robert Wells

- This book really helps children get an idea of relative size. It provides opportunities for students to look at the size of things in the world, beginning with the largest creature on earth, the blue whale. It is a great way to involve children in the concept of estimating. Opportunities to observe, compare, or predict the very biggest thing there is are plentiful.

Problem: Question related to the underpinning concepts in the selected text.
Instructional Approach: Independent Math—Math Discovery Hubs

Classroom Example in Action

LEAD BOOK: *How Big Is a Foot?*
READ AND DISCUSS: In a large group, read and discuss the story *How Big Is a Foot?*
ENGAGE: Provide opportunities for students to engage in the text.
POSE RELATED QUESTION: *How can you figure out what size the bed should be?*

Measurement Discovery Hub

Non-standard Units

MATH CENTRE #1 Activity
- **Materials**: a variety of non-standard measuring tools (e.g., straw, paper clips, string)
- Have students select five things to measure in the classroom.
- Have students measure the objects with straws, paper clips, and string and record their findings on a T-chart.
- Have students share with the larger group.

MATH CENTRE #2 Activity
- **Materials:** blank paper, pencil, scissors
- Read and discuss *How Big Is a Foot?*
- Have students use paper and pencil to trace around one of their feet.
- Have students use their foot pattern to measure the classroom.
- Have students share their results.
- Challenge students to find another way.

MATH CENTRE #3 Activity
- **Materials:** linked cubes, variety of objects
- Have students estimate the number of linked cubes it would take to measure the length and height of each object.
- Use a recording sheet to show the estimate and check to see how close you are to the actual number of linked cubes required.
- *Is there another way you could solve the problem?*
- Using pictures and words, show how you could solve the problem in a different way.

MATH CENTRE #4 Activity
- **Materials:** grid paper, markers
- Read and discuss *Measuring Up*.
- Take students to observe objects outdoors.
- Have students find five objects and measure them using their hands.
- Have students make a pictograph listing each object and drawing the number of hand spans used to measure the size of each object.
- Display their findings.

Linking Math Centre Activities and Assessment Strategies

Activity	Observation	Interview/ Conference	Portfolio	Self/Peer	Performance	Math Journal	Rubric	Checklist
1	✔							
2							✔	
3		✔			✔			
4		✔						

Recommended Books, Sample Activities, and a Suggested Process for Implementing the Measurement Strand

How Tall, How Short, How Far Away? by David Adler

SUMMARY: This book introduces students to a number of different measuring units that have been used over time—from cubits and spans to current customary and metric units. Adler incorporates hands-on activities within the text.

CONNECTING STRAND: Number Sense and Numeration

READ AND DISCUSS: *How Tall, How Short, How Far Away?*

POSE RELATED QUESTION: *Does it matter if we have standard measures? Why or why not?*

SAMPLE ACTIVITY: Have students measure an object in cubits, using the guide in the book, as well as in current customary or metric measures. Use the differences as a starting point for discussing the need for standard measures.

Pigs in the Pantry by Amy Axelrod

SUMMARY: Mrs. Pig isn't feeling well, so while she rests Mr. Pig and the two piglets decide to cook her a meal. The pigs follow a recipe as they make Firehouse Chili.

CONNECTING STRAND: Number Sense and Numeration

READ AND DISCUSS: *Pigs in the Pantry*

POSE RELATED QUESTION: *What did Mr. Pig and the two piglets forget to do before they started to cook?*

SAMPLE ACTIVITY: Have students work in small groups to choose a recipe from the school cookbook. Challenge each group to find out how the ingredients would need to be modified to make enough of the recipe for the class. Invite students to share their information with the class. Challenge each group to share the measuring tools they would need to measure the different ingredients.

It's Time by Kari Gold

SUMMARY: Gold begins with a question, "How can you tell the time of day?" and invites children to interact with the text through questions that focus on many facets in the development of the concept of time. This book includes photos of analog and digital clocks and challenges children to think about time in a real-world context.

CONNECTING STRAND: Number Sense and Numeration

READ AND DISCUSS: *It's Time*

POSE RELATED QUESTION: *How many ways is time used in your daily life?*

SAMPLE ACTIVITY: A clock is not the only way we can tell time. Have students make a poster demonstrating a variety of alternative ways we can use to tell time.

Short, Tall, Big or Small by Kari Gold

SUMMARY: Gold introduces math language in this concept book, strengthening the language arts and mathematics connections. Big, small, short, tall, heavy, light—Gold combines the language of mathematics with large colored photos of animals in the wild.

CONNECTING STRAND: Number Sense and Numeration

READ AND DISCUSS: *Short, Tall, Big or Small*

POSE RELATED QUESTION: *Is it important to know the language of mathematics? Why?*

SAMPLE ACTIVITY: Have students work in small groups to make a page for a big book showing a contrasting word pair. Make sure students include the words in their design. Create a cooperative class math language book.

Great Estimations by Bruce Goldstone

SUMMARY: A good introduction to estimation. Goldstone combines meaningful text, colorful illustrations, and key questioning to focus attention on how to estimate close to the real number. This book goes beyond estimating jellybeans. Children engage in a number of interactive challenges to strengthen their understanding of the concept.

CONNECTING STRAND: Number Sense and Numeration

READ AND DISCUSS: *Great Estimations*

POSE RELATED QUESTION: *What one strategy do you feel works well for you when you are estimating?*

SAMPLE ACTIVITY: Pose a question to students: *Suppose you had to estimate the number of jellybeans in a jar. How would you go about doing that?* Have them model the method

Goldstone demonstrates in the book. Have students describe how exactly you would go about estimating the number of jellybeans in the jar.

Twelve Snails to One Lizard by Susan Hightower

SUMMARY: This is the humorous story of Milo Beaver and Bubba Bullfrog. They are trying to measure a log to patch a hole in the dam. Milo doesn't know how long a log should be. Bullfrog tells Milo "an inch is about as long as a snail, and a foot is about as long as a lizard." A lighthearted tale that helps children understand the concept of non-standard linear measurement.

CONNECTING STRAND: Number Sense and Numeration

READ AND DISCUSS: *Twelve Snails to One Lizard*

POSE RELATED QUESTION: *If it takes a log measuring one snail and two lizard lengths to patch the hole in the dam, how many snail and lizard lengths would you need to measure the length of a log twice the size?*

SAMPLE ACTIVITY: Make available a number of different-sized objects. Have students measure the various lengths of the objects using snail and lizard lengths.

Is It Larger? Is It Smaller? by Tana Hoban

SUMMARY: This wordless book explores relative sizes through photographs of real objects. Hoban introduces young children to examples of big and small in the real world.

CONNECTING STRAND: Number Sense and Numeration

READ AND DISCUSS: *Is It Larger? Is It Smaller?*

POSE RELATED QUESTION: *How accurately can you estimate the size of an object?*

SAMPLE ACTIVITY: Ask students to list real-life objects in their environment. Have students estimate the size of each object and measure the objects using non-standard and standard units.

A Second Is a Hiccup by Hazel Hutchins

SUMMARY: Hutchins explains the concept of time, from seconds to hours, on both analog and digital clocks… and from years to millennia on the calendar.

CONNECTING STRAND: Number Sense and Numeration

READ AND DISCUSS: *A Second Is a Hiccup*

POSE RELATED QUESTION: *If a second is a hiccup, what might you think of to represent a minute?*

SAMPLE ACTIVITY: In small groups, have students brainstorm a number of ways they could demonstrate a minute. Have each group decide on the best way and act it out.

The Fattest, Tallest Snowman Ever by Bettina Ling

SUMMARY: The children in this story try to measure the snowmen with their arms to see whose snowman is the biggest. Their arms prove too short to measure around the snowmen, so they decide to use a string of paper clips instead. Ling introduces the reader to the concept of measuring objects using non-standard units and instruments, for example, paper clips, string.

CONNECTING STRAND: Number Sense and Numeration

READ AND DISCUSS: *The Fattest, Tallest Snowman Ever*

POSE RELATED QUESTION: *If you had to measure around the snowmen to see which was the biggest, would it be a good idea to estimate the distance around the snowmen first? Why?*

SAMPLE ACTIVITY: Ask students to estimate how many paper clips they might need to measure classroom objects. Have them then measure classroom objects using paper-clip chains. Provide charts for students to record their guess and the actual number of paper clips used to measure each object.

Classroom Object	My Guess	Actual Number of Paper Clips
Pencil case		
Book		
Desktop		

Have students build a chain, recording the number of paper clips and the length of the chain in a table. Write a rule to describe the pattern observed in the table.

Betcha! – Estimating by Stuart J. Murphy

SUMMARY: This book focuses on estimating and features two young friends who challenge each other to come up with the correct answers on determining such quantities as the number of jellybeans in the jar. At the end of the book are suggestions for adults and children to try other estimating activities.

CONNECTING STRAND: Data Management and Probability

READ AND DISCUSS: *Betcha!–Estimating*

POSE RELATED QUESTION: *Why is it important to estimate?*

SAMPLE ACTIVITY: Fill a number of jars with different quantities. Provide a same set of jars to each group of students. Have each group estimate the quantity of objects in each jar. The groups take turns presenting their estimations. Select individual students to make an accurate count of the objects in each jar.

How Big Is a Foot? by Rolf Myllar

SUMMARY: No one in the Kingdom knows the answer to this question: The king wants to give the queen a special bed for her birthday and measures the size using his own foot. He gives the measurements to the carpenter, who gives them to the little apprentice. When the little apprentice builds the bed, he uses his own feet as a standard, and the bed is too small. This story is an excellent source to use with children who are beginning to learn about measurement. It enables them to see that there is a need for standard units of measure in the world.

CONNECTING STRAND: Number Sense and Numeration

READ AND DISCUSS: *How Big Is a Foot?*

POSE RELATED QUESTION: *What advice could you give to the apprentice to help him solve the problem?*

SAMPLE ACTIVITY: Have students make tracings of their own feet. Make a graphic illustration of the concepts covered in this book.

Have students measure the dimensions of the classroom using their own feet. Use the different measures as a way to discuss the need for standard units. Have students consider how the size of the unit affects the number of units needed.

Units of Measure by Jennifer Osborne

SUMMARY: Osborne introduces children to the metric system using text and illustrations that bring meaning to vocabulary. This book focuses the reader's attention on the use of the metric system in found materials and real-life applications. Throughout this big book, Osborne poses the question "Which unit of measurement do you propose?"

CONNECTING STRAND: Number Sense and Numeration

READ AND DISCUSS: *Units of Measure*

POSE RELATED QUESTION: *Which unit of measurement would you choose?*

SAMPLE ACTIVITY: Display pictures of a variety of things in the environment. Have students sort and classify the pictures into which unit of measurement they would propose.

Measuring Up by Jennifer Osborne

SUMMARY: Measuring tapes adorn the cover of this big book, setting an early context. This concept book begins with non-standard units (e.g., feet, hand-to-hand) and progresses to standard units, introducing a variety of measurement tools—clock, thermometer, measuring tape, and cup. Osborne challenges children to make choices in selecting the right tool to suit its purpose. (e.g., "Which tool would you use to measure the length of a dog from nose to tail?") Children must choose from three measuring tools: measuring tape, paper clips, and ruler.

CONNECTING STRAND: Number Sense and Numeration

READ AND DISCUSS: *Measuring Up*

POSE RELATED QUESTION: *Which tool would you use to measure the length of a dog from nose to tail?*

SAMPLE ACTIVITY: Set up a measurement centre: *Which tool would you use?* Make a variety of measuring tools accessible. Create a number of challenging questions patterned on the example in the book. Have students take turns to draw a question from the box, read it aloud, and state the tool they selected and why.

Millions to Measure by David Schwartz

SUMMARY: Marvelosissimo the Magician explains the development of standard units, and shows the simplicity of calculating length, height, weight, and volume using the metric system. A good focus on the metric system.

CONNECTING STRAND: Number Sense and Numeration

READ AND DISCUSS: *Millions to Measure*

POSE RELATED QUESTION: *Which device should we use to measure each standard unit?*

SAMPLE ACTIVITY: Make a set of cards accessible for each group of students with relevant vocabulary written on the cards to represent the standard units of measurement (length, height, weight, volume). Make available a box of measuring tools used to make appropriate measurements. In small groups, have students select a card and work together to choose the most appropriate measurement tool.

Is a Blue Whale the Biggest Thing There Is? by Robert Wells

SUMMARY: This book really helps children get an idea of relative size. It provides opportunities to look at the size of things in the world, beginning with the largest creature on earth, the blue whale. Opportunities to observe, compare, or predict the very biggest thing there is are plentiful. Sizes of objects on earth and throughout the galaxy are compared using the size of a blue whale.

- Helps young children come to grips with the idea of relative size.
- Introduces big numbers and place value.

CONNECTING STRAND: Number Sense and Numeration

READ AND DISCUSS: *Is a Blue Whale the Biggest Thing There Is?*

POSE RELATED QUESTION: *How many students' lengths would equal the length of a full-grown blue whale?*

SAMPLE ACTIVITY: Have students compare the sizes of the different planets in the solar system. *How long does light take to travel from the sun to the different planets? How long would it take the Space Shuttle to travel from Earth to the various planets and return home?*

In small groups, have students make comparisons of animals—such as the size of a shark compared with a whale—and be able to distinguish small from large.

Measurement – Literature/Math Manipulative Organizer

MATHEMATICAL PROCESSES

Problem Solving; Reasoning and Proving; Reflecting; Selecting Tools and Computational Strategies; Connecting; Representing; Communicating

Title/ Author	Concepts/Skills/Topics/Additional Comments	Literary Style/Type	Math Manipulatives/Found Materials
How Tall, How Short, How Far Away? David Adler	Metric measurement, different measuring units (cubits, spans), attributes, measurement relationships	Non-fiction	Concrete objects/tools for non-standard and standardized measurements
Pigs in the Pantry Amy Axelrod	Estimating, units of measurement, measurement relationships	Fiction	Standardized measuring tools (cup, spoon), weigh scale
It's Time Kari Gold	Second, minute, hour, real-world applications, measurement relationships, units	Non-fiction (big book)–concept book	Clocks–analog, digital
Short, Tall, Big or Small Kari Gold	Math language (*big, small, short, wide, tall, heavy, light,* etc.), real-life application, attributes, measurement sense, measurement relationships	Non-fiction (big book)–concept book	Digital camera
Great Estimations Bruce Goldstone	Capacity, estimating and finding actual count, units, measurement sense	Non-fiction	Concrete objects
Twelve Snails to One Lizard Susan Hightower	Non-standard units of measurement, standard units of measurement, measurement relationships	Fiction	Objects for measuring non-standard units, measurement tools for standardized units of measurement
Is It Larger? Is It Smaller? Tana Hoban	Estimating size of objects, units, measurement sense, attributes, real-world connection–stunning photographs	Fiction–wordless book	Standard unit measuring tools
A Second Is a Hiccup Hazel Hutchins	Units of time (second, minute, hour, day, week, month, year), measurement sense, units, measurement relationships	Fiction	Clocks–analog, digital
The Fattest, Tallest Snowman Ever Bettina Ling	Non-standard units, follow-up measuring activities, attributes, measurement sense	Fiction	Non-standard measuring tools: string, paper clips
Betcha! – Estimating Stuart J. Murphy	Estimating, measuring sense	Fiction	Variety of measuring tools
How Big Is a Foot? Rolf Myllar	Non-standard, standardized measurement–length, units, measurement sense, measurement relationships	Fiction–fable	Tools to measure length–rulers, measuring tapes, etc.
Units of Measure *Measuring Up* Jennifer Osborne	Non-standard/standard, units, measurement sense	Non-fiction (big book)–concept book	String, paper clips, ruler, tape measures
Millions to Measure David Schwartz	Standardized units, metric system—length, height, volume; history of measurement, attributes, measurement relationships	Fiction	Standard measurement tools
Is a Blue Whale the Biggest Thing There Is? Robert Wells	Measurement in relation to size of objects, estimation, comparisons, measurement sense, measurement relationships	Non-fiction	Visualization

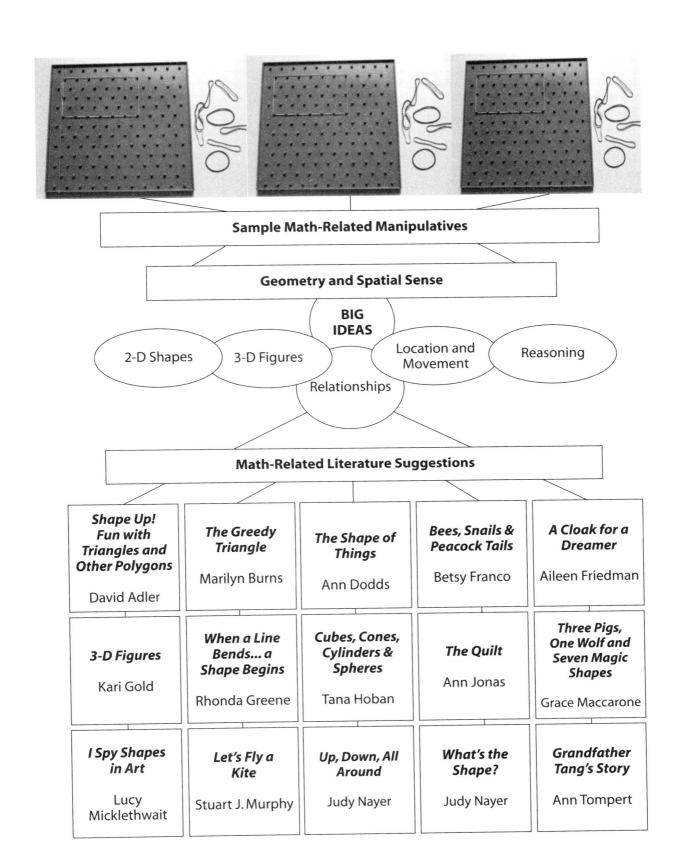

Sample Math-Related Manipulatives

Geometry and Spatial Sense

BIG IDEAS

2-D Shapes

3-D Figures

Location and Movement

Reasoning

Relationships

Math-Related Literature Suggestions

Shape Up! Fun with Triangles and Other Polygons David Adler	*The Greedy Triangle* Marilyn Burns	*The Shape of Things* Ann Dodds	*Bees, Snails & Peacock Tails* Betsy Franco	*A Cloak for a Dreamer* Aileen Friedman
3-D Figures Kari Gold	*When a Line Bends... a Shape Begins* Rhonda Greene	*Cubes, Cones, Cylinders & Spheres* Tana Hoban	*The Quilt* Ann Jonas	*Three Pigs, One Wolf and Seven Magic Shapes* Grace Maccarone
I Spy Shapes in Art Lucy Micklethwait	*Let's Fly a Kite* Stuart J. Murphy	*Up, Down, All Around* Judy Nayer	*What's the Shape?* Judy Nayer	*Grandfather Tang's Story* Ann Tompert

Geometry and Spatial Sense

Reflecting on Antonia's memory: merely mentioning the word *geometry* to many elementary school teachers brings back memories of high-school geometry that dealt with abstraction and proof.

The Big Ideas of the Geometry and Spatial Sense strand include properties of 2-D shapes, properties of 3-D figures, geometric relationships, location and movement, and geometric reasoning. Many opportunities and experiences reflect more than one Big Idea. Geometric learning begins with sorting and classifying 2-D shapes and 3-D figures by attributes, recognizing symmetry, relating shapes to other shapes, and designing and describing location using positional language. The strand progresses to using a reference tool to identify right angles, relating different types of quadrilaterals, recognizing transformations… and more. The mathematical processes—problem solving, reasoning and proving, reflecting, selecting tools and computational strategies, connecting, representing, and communicating—are integrated throughout. In the primary grades, geometric representations manifest themselves in drawings that come in handy when exploring and investigating a variety of real-life problems.

Geometry is all around us, from the shapes in buildings to the 2-D and 3-D objects in a small child's toy box. Children develop spatial sense as they familiarize themselves with their surroundings and the objects in those surroundings. Literature can promote young children's developing understanding of geometric concepts. As teachers, we can use books such as Judy Nayer's *Up, Down, All Around* to extend young children's knowledge and understanding of relative position in space. Stories, ongoing dialog, and hands-on exploration work together to strengthen spatial sense. Students learn about symmetry, congruence, perimeter, and area through hands-on exploration and investigation of manipulative materials. For example, block building helps children develop spatial sense. They learn about basic shapes and three-dimensional figures when playing with blocks. Providing opportunities for experience in all these geometric areas—using prompts and guided questioning—helps students make sense of the geometry in everyday life. For example, questions such as "How are all the shapes alike?" and guided inquiring such as "Share the directions for building the structure you just made with blocks" work together to strengthen a student's knowledge and understanding of Geometry and Spatial Sense.

Classroom Implementation – Preplanning

STRAND: Geometry and Spatial Sense
BIG IDEA: 2-D Shapes
KEY CONCEPTS/SKILLS: Identify, compare, classify 2-D shapes and 3-D figures, exploring, sorting, classifying, constructing geometric shapes
ASSESSMENT STRATEGY: Per Assessment Chart
TEXT SET: Select *relevant* Big Idea Text Set.

Big Idea Text Set – Linking Math Manipulatives and Math-Related Literature

2-D Shapes

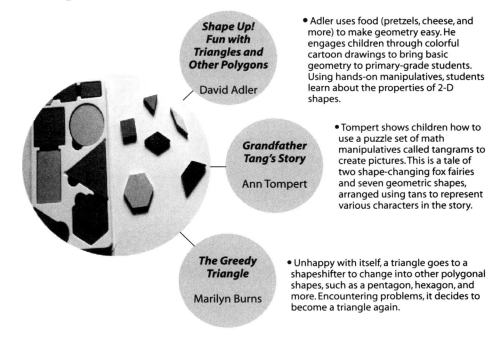

Shape Up! Fun with Triangles and Other Polygons

David Adler

- Adler uses food (pretzels, cheese, and more) to make geometry easy. He engages children through colorful cartoon drawings to bring basic geometry to primary-grade students. Using hands-on manipulatives, students learn about the properties of 2-D shapes.

Grandfather Tang's Story

Ann Tompert

- Tompert shows children how to use a puzzle set of math manipulatives called tangrams to create pictures. This is a tale of two shape-changing fox fairies and seven geometric shapes, arranged using tans to represent various characters in the story.

The Greedy Triangle

Marilyn Burns

- Unhappy with itself, a triangle goes to a shapeshifter to change into other polygonal shapes, such as a pentagon, hexagon, and more. Encountering problems, it decides to become a triangle again.

Problem: Question related to the underpinning concepts in the selected text.
Instructional Approach: Independent Math—Math Discovery Hubs

Classroom Example in Action

LEAD BOOK: *The Greedy Triangle*
READ AND DISCUSS: In a large group, read the book *The Greedy Triangle*.
ENGAGE: Provide opportunities for students to engage in the text.
POSE RELATED QUESTION: *Is there a downside to the triangle becoming a pentagon?*

Geometry and Spatial Sense Discovery Hub

2-D Shapes

Math Centre #1 Activity
- **Materials:** pattern blocks
- Read *Shape Up!* again.
- *What's the shape?* Discuss shapes.
- Have students sort the pattern blocks into various 2-D shapes.
- Ask students to create a bar graph showing how many shapes there are in each category.

Math Centre #2 Activity
- **Materials:** geoboards, rubber bands
- Have students work in partners to make a triangle, a pentagon, a hexagon, and so on.
- Do a Gallery Walk in which the students walk around to other groups to observe the different shapes.
  - Students guess the names of the other groups' shapes.

Math Centre #3 Activity
- **Materials:** digital camera
- Share the big book *What's the Shape?* by Judy Nayer.
- Discuss 2-D shapes in the real world.
- In groups, have students create their own photo book identifying shapes in the real world.

Math Centre #4 Activity
- **Materials:** tangram kits
- Using the tangram kits, have students put the pieces together to form a square.
- Encourage students to make other shapes using the tangrams. Have them share with others.

OTHER GEOMETRY BOOK SUGGESTIONS

Thong, Roseanne. *Round Is a Mooncake: A Book of Shapes.*
Emberley, Ed. *The Wing on a Flea: A Book About Shapes*
Hutchins, Pat. *Changes, Changes.*
Carle, Eric. *Draw Me a Star.*

Linking Math Centre Activities and Assessment Strategies

Activity	Observation	Interview/ Conference	Portfolio	Self/Peer	Performance	Math Journal	Rubric	Checklist
1						✔		
2	✔							
3							✔	
4				✔				

Recommended Books, Sample Activities, and a Suggested Process for Implementing the Geometry and Spatial Sense Strand

Shape Up! Fun with Triangles and Other Polygons by David Adler

SUMMARY: A good introduction to triangles and other polygons.

CONNECTING STRAND: Data Management and Probability

READ AND DISCUSS: *Shape Up!*

POSE RELATED QUESTION: *What are the attributes of the various polygons listed in the book?*

SAMPLE ACTIVITY: So that students can demonstrate their knowledge of shapes and their properties, provide a variety of concrete materials for them to construct various polygons.

The Greedy Triangle by Marilyn Burns

SUMMARY: A good introduction to polygons. The triangle goes to see a shapeshifter to change into other polygonal shapes, only to return to the shapeshifter to become a triangle again. Throughout this tale, children meet shapes that are more complex: pentagon, hexagon, quadrilateral.

CONNECTING STRAND: Patterning and Algebra

READ AND DISCUSS: *The Greedy Triangle*

POSE RELATED QUESTION: *What are some examples of polygons found in natural and artificial objects?*

SAMPLE ACTIVITY: Make geoboard and rubber bands available to students. Have students create a polygon design on a geoboard using a variety of polygons. Students take turns guessing the name and number of polygons in each other's shape.

The Shape of Things by Ann Dodds

SUMMARY: Dodds introduces children to geometric shapes found in the world around us. Throughout the story, children are engaged in finding, for example, all the triangles in the illustrations. Shape patterns form a border on each page, encouraging ongoing dialog about shapes, color, and size.

CONNECTING STRAND: Patterning and Algebra

READ AND DISCUSS: *The Shape of Things*

POSE RELATED QUESTION: *How many other shapes can you find in the illustrations?*

SAMPLE ACTIVITY: Provide a large quantity of concrete materials for students to explore 2-D shapes. Have students create a shape museum where their shapes will be put on display in the classroom.

Bees, Snails & Peacock Tails by Betsy Franco

SUMMARY: Through text and colorful illustrations, Franco helps students explore and investigate the hidden shapes and patterns in nature. From observing a peacock tail to a beehive, Franco draws attention to shapes and their natural connections in the real world.

CONNECTING STRAND: Patterning and Algebra

READ AND DISCUSS: *Bees, Snails & Peacock Tails*

POSE RELATED QUESTION: *What shapes in nature can you find in the schoolyard?*

SAMPLE ACTIVITY: Have students take a digital photo of a shape they find in the schoolyard. Invite them to create a shape poster. Students glue the photo on the poster and draw a background to hide their shape. Challenge students to guess the hidden shape. Have students make a poster gallery of all the shapes. Hold a poster walkthrough.

A Cloak for the Dreamer by Aileen Friedman

SUMMARY: A tailor's sons are charged with making a cloak to keep out the wind and the rain. Friedman describes how the sons make patchworks of rectangles, triangles, and squares. The reader is naturally drawn into exploring and investigating ways to combine, dissect, and transform shapes.

CONNECTING STRAND: Measurement

READ AND DISCUSS: *A Cloak for the Dreamer*

POSE RELATED QUESTION: *Which regular polygons tessellate? Why?*

SAMPLE ACTIVITY: Following an exploration and investigation of ways to combine, dissect, and transform shapes, have students use pattern blocks to create their own tessellations.

3-D Figures by Kari Gold

SUMMARY: Colorful illustrations introduce 3-D figures and related math vocabulary. Through direct questioning, Gold draws the reader to a variety of pictures of 3-D figures with linkages to the identified solids. Throughout the book, children discover these figures in the environment. For example, the cylinder is found in the structure of a lighthouse. Gold continues to broaden children's understanding of these figures by challenging them to find the 3-D figures embedded in pictures from different parts of the world.

CONNECTING STRAND: Patterning and Algebra

READ AND DISCUSS: *3-D Figures*

POSE RELATED QUESTION: *What other 3-D figures are located in your community?*

SAMPLE ACTIVITY: Have students take turns reaching into a bag to select a three-dimensional object without looking at it. Play a game in which students take turns guessing what the object might be. Have students tell what properties make up their 3-D figure.

When a Line Bends... a Shape Begins by Rhonda Greene

SUMMARY: The rhyming text of this story explains how simple lines create basic shapes. Greene lays out descriptions of each geometric shape to form the shape discussed.

CONNECTING STRANDS: Patterning and Algebra, Number Sense and Numeration

READ AND DISCUSS: *When a Line Bends... a Shape Begins*

POSE RELATED QUESTION: *Is a rectangle a square? Explain your thinking.*

SAMPLE ACTIVITY: Connect mathematics with technology. Ask students to choose a shape and use their own words to describe its characteristics. Invite them to look for a real-world object that shares that shape. Have students take a digital photo of the object. Make a class geo photo album showing the shapes and their connections to real-world objects.

Cubes, Cones, Cylinders & Spheres by Tana Hoban

SUMMARY: This book includes all kinds of familiar objects in a variety of shapes, including cubes, cones, and spheres.

CONNECTING STRANDS: Data Management and Probability, Patterning and Algebra

READ AND DISCUSS: *Cubes, Cones, Cylinders & Spheres*

POSE RELATED QUESTION: *Can you find an object from the real world that has more than one shape in it?*

SAMPLE ACTIVITY: Invite students to go on a 3-D Expedition. Challenge them to find objects in the environment that represent 3-D shapes. Have students make pictorial graphs of their findings, showing what and how many 3-D objects are in each category.

The Quilt by Ann Jonas

SUMMARY: A child falls into a dream while clutching her new quilt. In her dream, she searches for a lost teddy bear in places that correspond to a patch of the quilt. Jonas introduces children to a variety of shapes in the context of story. She challenges them to find the patches on the quilt that relate to the dream.

CONNECTING STRAND: Patterning and Algebra

READ AND DISCUSS: *The Quilt*

POSE RELATED QUESTION: *How many different kinds of shapes are represented on each page?*

SAMPLE ACTIVITY: Read the story again. Have students work with partners to find and identify the shapes on each page. Students must design a square for a patchwork quilt and include at least three different shapes in their design. Encourage them to use their math journal to write about the properties of their shapes and tell why they chose these shapes for their design.

Three Pigs, One Wolf and Seven Magic Shapes by Grace Maccarone

SUMMARY: Maccarone introduces children to tangrams in a problem-solving context. The focus is on how three pigs use seven magic shapes to form solutions to various problems. An excellent book, providing children multiple opportunities to explore making shapes with tangram pieces.

CONNECTING STRANDS: Patterning and Algebra, Number Sense and Numeration

READ AND DISCUSS: *Three Pigs, One Wolf and Seven Magic Shapes*

POSE RELATED QUESTION: *What new tangram figures can you make?*

SAMPLE ACTIVITY: Challenge students to use the tangram kits to recreate the figures in the book. Provide opportunities to create their own tangram shapes. Have students choose their favorite shape and share orally with others. Take a digital photo of their shape and place a copy in their learning portfolios.

I Spy Shapes in Art by Lucy Micklethwait

SUMMARY: The "I Spy" format encourages children to find geometric shapes in each of fourteen paintings in the world of art appreciation.

CONNECTING STRAND: Patterning and Algebra

READ AND DISCUSS: *I Spy Shapes in Art*

POSE RELATED QUESTION: *Can you think of another way shapes are used in art?*

SAMPLE ACTIVITY: Have students play the "I Spy" game using 2-D shapes.

Let's Fly a Kite by Stuart J. Murphy

SUMMARY: Bob and Hannah learn about symmetry when kites they make fail to fly. Using the concept of symmetry, their babysitter finds a solution to each problem. Charming illustrations provide insight into the method used to divide everyday objects into two equal parts.

CONNECTING STRAND: Patterning and Algebra

READ AND DISCUSS: *Let's Fly a Kite*

POSE RELATED QUESTION: *Can you find examples of symmetry and non-symmetry in the real world?*

SAMPLE ACTIVITY: Have students make their own kite and use their math journal to explain the concept of symmetry as it relates to their model.

Up, Down, All Around by Judy Nayer

SUMMARY: Nayer employs highlighted words and large, colorful animal drawings to model mathematically related words in meaningful contexts. She uses questioning to draw out meaningful responses. For example, "Who's hanging 'upside down' without a care?" is accompanied by a drawing of two-toed sloths hanging upside down.

CONNECTING STRAND: Number Sense and Numeration

READ AND DISCUSS: *Up, Down, All Around*

POSE RELATED QUESTION: *Can you think of any other mathematical words you need to understand when working with 2-D shapes or 3-D figures?*

SAMPLE ACTIVITY: Have students work in small groups. One person from each group hides an object. Students provide clues using relevant mathematical vocabulary to help others find the object. Encourage students to take turns within their group to hide other objects.

What's the Shape? by Judy Nayer

SUMMARY: This big book provides an introduction to shapes in the environment. Pictures of the shapes form a band running along the bottom of each two-page spread.

CONNECTING STRAND: Patterning and Algebra

READ AND DISCUSS: *What's the Shape?*

POSE RELATED QUESTION: *What other objects can you think of from our environment that take on any one of the 2-D shapes at the bottom of the pages?*

SAMPLE ACTIVITY: Make available to students a variety of found materials (such as straws) and play clay for joiners. Have students make a variety of 2-D shapes. Encourage them to share their shapes with a partner.

Grandfather Tang's Story by Ann Tompert

SUMMARY: Tompert uses tangrams to spin a tale about two shape-changing fox fairies. Seven tans are manipulated to represent various characters in the story.

CONNECTING STRAND: Patterning and Algebra

READ AND DISCUSS: *Grandfather Tang's Story*

POSE RELATED QUESTION: *What other animals can you make using the tangram pieces?*

SAMPLE ACTIVITY: Make tangrams accessible to the students. Have partners create the animals from the story using the tans. Encourage students to make their own tangram animals.

Geometry and Spatial Sense – Literature/Math Manipulative Organizer

MATHEMATICAL PROCESSES

Problem Solving; Reasoning and Proving; Reflecting; Selecting Tools and Computational Strategies; Connecting; Representing; Communicating

Title/Author	Concepts/Skills/Topics/Additional Comments	Literary Style/Type	Math Manipulatives/Found Materials
Shape Up! Fun with Triangles and Other Polygons David Adler	2-D shapes–sorting, classifying by attributes	Non-fiction–concept book	Geostrips, stamp shapes, other concrete materials
The Greedy Triangle Marilyn Burns	Sides, angles, geometric 2-D shapes, geometric reasoning	Fiction–picture book	Geoboards, rubber bands, pattern blocks
The Shape of Things Ann Dodds	2-D shapes, real-world applications, sorting, classifying	Fiction–story, rhyming text	Geostrips, stamp shape set
Bees, Snails & Peacock Tails Betsy Franco	Shapes in the environment, classifying, real-world applications	Fiction–story	Digital camera, working materials
A Cloak for the Dreamer Aileen Friedman	Shapes, angles, patterning, tessellations, multicultural	Fiction–story	Pattern blocks
3-D Figures Kari Gold	Sorting, classifying	Non-fiction–concept book	3-D solids–polydrons, frameworks, geoblocks
When a Line Bends… a Shape Begins Rhonda Greene	Shapes in nature, real-world applications, geometric relationships	Picture book–rhyming text	Digital camera, photo album
Cubes, Cones, Cylinders & Spheres Tana Hoban	3-D shapes, real-world applications, geometric relationships, observation	Non-fiction–concept book	Geoblocks, d-stix, solid sets
The Quilt Ann Jonas	2-D shapes, observation, sorting, classifying	Fiction–picture book	Variety of working materials
Three Pigs, One Wolf and Seven Magic Shapes Grace Maccarone	2-D shapes, problem solving, location and movement, observation	Fiction–story	Tangram kit
I Spy Shapes in Art Lucy Micklethwait	Observation, real-world applications, interdisciplinary connections	Non-fiction	2-D shapes
Let's Fly a Kite Stuart J. Murphy	2-D shapes, observation, recognizing symmetry	Fiction–story	Symmetry shapes
Up, Down, All Around Judy Nayer	2-D shapes, 3-D figures, observation, sorting, classification	Non-fiction–big book (read-aloud)	Variety of 2-D and 3-D shapes, hands-on materials
What's the Shape? Judy Nayer	Observations, sorting, classifying, real-world applications, 2-D shapes	Non-fiction–big book	Related found materials
Grandfather Tang's Story Ann Tompert	Relating shapes to other shapes, observation, multicultural	Fiction–story, folktale	Tangram kit

Sample Math-Related Manipulatives

Patterning and Algebra

Patterns and Relationships	**BIG IDEAS**	Expressions and Equality

Math-Related Literature Suggestions

Rooster's Off to See the World Eric Carle	*The Very Hungry Caterpillar* Eric Carle	*Five Little Monkeys Jumping on the Bed* Eileen Christelow	*The House That Jack Built* Elizabeth Falconer	*Each Orange Had 8 Slices* Paul Giganti
Skip-Counting Kari Gold	*What Comes Next?* Kari Gold	*The Doorbell Rang* Pat Hutchins	*Patterns All Around Me* Trisha Jones	*Arithme-tickle: An Even Number of Odd Riddle Rhymes* Patrick Lewis
A Pair of Socks Stuart J. Murphy	*One Hundred Hungry Ants* Elinor J. Pinczes	*The Button Box* Margarette S. Reid	*Lots and Lots of Zebra Stripes* Stephen Swinburne	*Math for All Seasons* Greg Tang

Patterning and Algebra

The Patterning and Algebra strand focuses on the concepts of Patterns and Relationships and Equality as outlined in the graphic organizer. The concept of Patterns and Relationships includes identifying, describing, analyzing a variety of patterns (repeating, growing, shrinking). Repeating patterns such as ABABABAB, AABCAABC play themselves out in songs and clapping and snapping patterns where students identify the pattern and repeat it. Growing patterns (e.g., ABCAABCAAABC or 5,7,9,11), where one variable changes in the pattern, are more difficult for students to understand. The duality of increasing or decreasing by a constant amount makes this patterning concept more complex. Understanding growing patterns begins in the early years, during which young children explore and investigate linking cubes. Teachers can observe them stacking cubes in towers and lining up the towers in order of size. Patterns can be represented in a variety of ways, for example, numerical, graphic, algebraic, and geometric. At the upper end of the early years, the patterning concept expands to include describing, extending, and creating a variety of numeric and geometric patterns. Students learn to sort, classify, and order objects by size, number, and other properties. Their understanding of patterns, relations, and functions is reinforced through questioning—for example, "Is there a pattern to the number of petals on flowers?"—as they learn and grow to represent and analyze patterns and functions, using words, tables, and graphs. Teachers can provide opportunities for children to understand the various types of patterns through observation, experimentation, and discovery.

The concept of equality begins with children using concrete materials to demonstrate an understanding of the concept. At the early level of the developmental continuum, have students use concrete materials, symbols, and addition and subtraction up to 18 to demonstrate their understanding of equality. At the upper end of the early years, have students demonstrate the concept of equality between pairs of expressions, using addition and subtraction of one-and two-digit numbers. The introduction and use of pan balance scales encourages children to use and understand math-related language: *equal/not equal, same/different, balanced/unbalanced*. Activities such as linking cubes to make towers that are equal in quantity (height) help to build algebraic thinking.

Using children's literature to integrate algebraic thinking provides a forum for students to remember the story and its related investigation and in turn remember the mathematics. Questions such as, "How did you arrive at your pattern?" and "What does this pattern, or relationship, remind you of?" serve to facilitate the kind of classroom discourse that builds students' algebraic thinking skills. (Soares, June, et al. 2006. "Thinking Algebraically Across the Elementary School Curriculum." *Teaching Children Mathematics.*) There is an abundance of children's literature that speaks to the development of these concepts. For example, Greg Tang's *Math for All Seasons* gives a terrific impetus for students to find patterns and use patterns to solve math problems quickly. Building on this, Tang's book helps children see additional ways in which finding patterns is useful. Children learn to pair or group items to make adding easier, subtract to add (e.g., two 5s are 10 minus 2 equals 8), and to look for patterns and symmetries that provide further shortcuts to addition. Tang invites children to recognize visual groupings (twos, threes, and fives) to make adding faster and more accurate.

Preschoolers have engaged in algebraic thinking from the cradle onward. They listen to the metrical patterns of poems and stories told in simple verse and rhyme, the recitation of the days of the week, and join in chanting the refrains. The repetition of phrases in the text introduces patterns and helps them understand the concept of patterning. There are numerous connections to language arts in mathematics education. Well-known children's stories such as *Brown Bear, Brown Bear; The Gingerbread Boy; Little Red Riding Hood;* and *The Three Billy Goats Gruff* come to mind. These tales are rich in patterns and symbols, and provide opportunities to explore and investigate patterns and relationships.

I'm reminded of a cold, crisp, snowy morning in Vermont with my grandson, who was two at the time. He loved the story of the Three Billy Goats Gruff and wanted to hear it read over and over, again and again. This vacation property was a perfect setting to act out the story in which three billy goats cross a bridge, under which awaits a fearsome troll who tries to prevent them from crossing. There was an old wooden bridge on the property with just enough room for the fearsome troll to hide. My grandson played the role of the three billy goats and that meant I was to be the fearsome troll. As my grandson trip-trapped over the bridge, I called out, "Who's that tripping over my bridge?" He would squeal, "Oh, it is only I, the tiniest Billy Goat Gruff." As we acted out the whole story, my grandson couldn't wait to repeat the refrain. Young children identify with characters and situations, engaging in rhythmic chants and nonsensical verses. The Vermont experience reinforced for me the notion that the study of patterns and relationships begins very early in a child's informal schooling. Reading stories and poems that include repetitive patterns along with posing questions—"What do you see?" "What's different?"—help focus students' attention on finding, describing, and using word patterns.

Repetitive songs, such as *B-I-N-G-O* and *I Know an Old Lady Who Swallowed a Fly*, and finger plays are built around repeating and growing patterns engaging students into the world of patterning. Encourage students to listen and join in clapping, stamping, or snapping their fingers to the pattern. Young children recognize, repeat, compare, and manipulate patterns in their understanding of mathematics. Invite children to work in small groups to create their own rhythmic pattern. Repeated opportunities to work with word/number patterns lead to the concept of functions in mathematics. For a number of years, primary teachers have engaged their students in algebraic thinking. Primary teachers have been building a good algebraic foundation where students must recognize, describe, and generalize patterns. There appears to be reluctance, however, to formalize algebra as one of the strands addressed in the Early Years. Research conducted by Zalman Usiskin confirms this attitude. "To many teachers, introducing algebra in the primary grades is the epitome of working with mathematical concepts too early, before students are ready." (Usiskin, Zalman. Feb. 1997. "Doing Algebra in Grades K–4." *Teaching Children Mathematics.*) Knowing and understanding the developmental continuum of the concept of patterns aids in making good instructional decisions. Questions such as "When do I introduce the concept of patterns?" "What is the next step?" and so on naturally arise when planning a mathematics program. Following is a Developmental Continuum of Learning in Algebra for use in the primary grades. Reflect on it and use it as a guide when you are selecting the literature to support the development of the concept of patterns.

A Developmental Continuum of Learning in Algebra in the Primary Grades

The Concept of Patterns

K	1	2	3
Introduce word/ number patterns. e.g., ABAB	Repeating Patterns using one attribute.	Repeating, growing, and shrinking patterns. e.g., 2,4,6,8	Extending growing and shrinking patterns. Representing geometric patterns with a number sequence, number line, and a bar graph.

The Concept of Equality

K	1	2	3
Using concrete materials.	Using concrete materials, and addition and subtraction to 10.	Using concrete materials, symbols, and addition and subtraction to 18.	Using addition and subtraction of one- and two-digit numbers.

Classroom Implementation – Preplanning

STRAND: Patterning and Algebra

BIG IDEA: Finding, Describing, and Using Patterns

KEY CONCEPTS/SKILLS: Word/number patterns, repeating, growing and shrinking patterns, extending growing patterns, representing geometric patterns with number line and bar graph

ASSESSMENT STRATEGY: Per Assessment Chart

TEXT SET: Create *relevant* Big Idea Text Set.

Big Idea Text Set – Linking Math Manipulatives and Math-Related Literature

Patterning

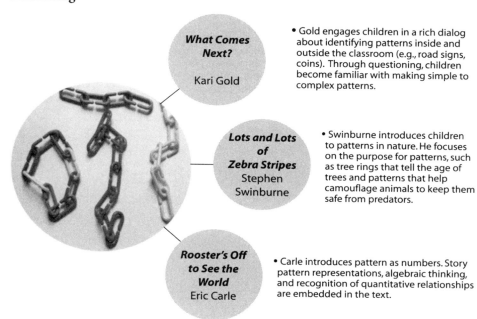

What Comes Next?

Kari Gold

• Gold engages children in a rich dialog about identifying patterns inside and outside the classroom (e.g., road signs, coins). Through questioning, children become familiar with making simple to complex patterns.

Lots and Lots of Zebra Stripes
Stephen Swinburne

• Swinburne introduces children to patterns in nature. He focuses on the purpose for patterns, such as tree rings that tell the age of trees and patterns that help camouflage animals to keep them safe from predators.

Rooster's Off to See the World
Eric Carle

• Carle introduces pattern as numbers. Story pattern representations, algebraic thinking, and recognition of quantitative relationships are embedded in the text.

Problem: Question related to the underpinning concepts in the selected text.
Instructional Approach: Independent Math—Math Discovery Hubs

Classroom Example in Action

LEAD BOOK: *What Comes Next?*

READ AND DISCUSS: In a large group, read the big book *What Comes Next?*

ENGAGE: Provide opportunities for students to engage in the text. Questions such as "Tell me what you were thinking." and "Did you solve this a different way?" reveal students' thinking and prompt them to justify, explain, and build arguments—processes that lie at the heart of algebraic reasoning. (Blanton, Maria and James Kaput. 2003. "Developing Elementary Teachers' Algebra Eyes and Ears." *Teaching Children Mathematics.*)

POSE RELATED QUESTION: *What kind of pattern do you see?*

Patterning and Algebra Discovery Hub

Patterning

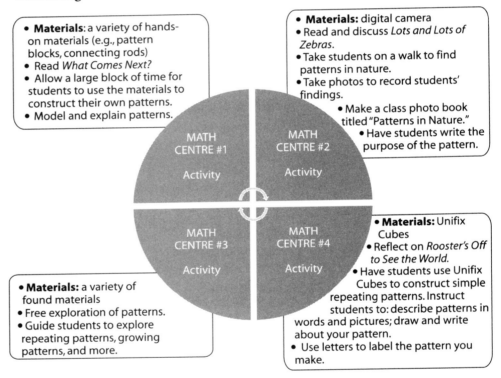

- **Materials**: a variety of hands-on materials (e.g., pattern blocks, connecting rods)
- Read *What Comes Next?*
- Allow a large block of time for students to use the materials to construct their own patterns.
- Model and explain patterns.

MATH CENTRE #1 Activity

- **Materials**: digital camera
- Read and discuss *Lots and Lots of Zebras*.
- Take students on a walk to find patterns in nature.
- Take photos to record students' findings.
- Make a class photo book titled "Patterns in Nature."
- Have students write the purpose of the pattern.

MATH CENTRE #2 Activity

- **Materials**: a variety of found materials
- Free exploration of patterns.
- Guide students to explore repeating patterns, growing patterns, and more.

MATH CENTRE #3 Activity

- **Materials:** Unifix Cubes
- Reflect on *Rooster's Off to See the World*.
- Have students use Unifix Cubes to construct simple repeating patterns. Instruct students to: describe patterns in words and pictures; draw and write about your pattern.
- Use letters to label the pattern you make.

MATH CENTRE #4 Activity

OTHER PATTERNING BOOK SUGGESTIONS

Hoban, Tana. *Is it Red? Is it Yellow? Is it Blue?*
Patilla, Peter. *Sorting.*
Tang, Greg. *Math Appeal.*

Linking Math Centre Activities and Assessment Strategies

Activity	Observation	Interview/ Conference	Portfolio	Self/Peer	Performance	Math Journal	Rubric	Checklist
1					✔			
2						✔		
3	✔							
4			✔					

Recommended Books, Sample Activities, and a Suggested Process for Implementing the Patterning and Algebra Strand

Rooster's Off to See the World by Eric Carle

SUMMARY: Children engage in the text as Carle takes them on a trip with the rooster and his friends. The rooster is joined by two cats, three frogs, four turtles, five fish, offering a graphic introduction to the meaning of patterning and numbers. The symbols in the corner of each spread help readers keep track of the travellers' growing number. Graphic and number patterns abound.

CONNECTING STRANDS: Number Sense and Numeration, Data Management and Probability

READ AND DISCUSS: Rooster's Off to See the World

POSE RELATED QUESTION: What does this pattern remind you of?

SAMPLE ACTIVITY: Have students create a new story based on a growing pattern. Make available concrete materials such as Unifix Cubes to help students create their pattern. Allow time for students to act out their story.

The Very Hungry Caterpillar by Eric Carle

SUMMARY: Carle introduces the names of fruits and counting to ten as the caterpillar eats through different foods each day. This book provides many opportunities for patterning. Growing patterns, cyclical patterns (the names of the days of the week), repeated language patterns, and the cycle implicit in the metamorphosis of a butterfly are embedded in the story.

CONNECTING STRANDS: Number Sense and Numeration, Data Management and Probability

READ AND DISCUSS: The Very Hungry Caterpillar

POSE RELATED QUESTION: What kind of pattern do you see? How do you know?

SAMPLE ACTIVITY: To earmark the stages implicit in the lifecycle of a human, have students make the lifecycle stages of a human, using real photos at various points in their life.

Five Little Monkeys Jumping on the Bed by Eileen Christelow

SUMMARY: Christelow's simple rhyming text with its focus on numbers from 1 to 5 introduces the concept of number in a repeated growing and shrinking pattern context.

CONNECTING STRAND: Number Sense and Numeration

READ AND DISCUSS: Five Little Monkeys Jumping on the Bed

POSE RELATED QUESTION: If there were seven little monkeys jumping on the bed, would the pattern be different? In what way?

SAMPLE ACTIVITY: Have students use a different number and a different animal to create their own story on a growing and shrinking pattern. Have students repeat their growing and shrinking pattern, drawing their story in picture format. Encourage students to act out their story.

The House That Jack Built by Elizabeth Falconer

SUMMARY: Falconer describes a growing pattern from the house that Jack built to the farmer who sows corn.
CONNECTING STRANDS: Number Sense and Numeration, Data Management and Probability
READ AND DISCUSS: *The House That Jack Built*
POSE RELATED QUESTION: *In what way is patterning used in this story? How do you know?*
SAMPLE ACTIVITY: Have students use math manipulatives to create repeating and growing patterns.

Each Orange Had 8 Slices by Paul Giganti

SUMMARY: A wonderful book to use in patterning, multiplication, and creative thinking. Dynamic illustrations and appealing words combine to introduce patterning and relationships as well as reinforcing visual literacy. An excellent counting book as well.
CONNECTING STRAND: Number Sense and Numeration
READ AND DISCUSS: *Each Orange Had 8 Slices*
POSE RELATED QUESTION: *What do your findings make you wonder?*
SAMPLE ACTIVITY: Make available pattern blocks for students to repeat the patterning cycle from the book. Have students make their own patterns using the pattern blocks. Encourage them to share their patterning scheme with a friend.

Skip-Counting by Kari Gold

SUMMARY: An excellent big book introducing skip counting. Beautiful illustrations provide meaningful understanding of the concept. The text engages children to inquire and respond throughout the sharing of this book.
CONNECTING STRAND: Number Sense and Numeration
READ AND DISCUSS: *Skip-Counting*
POSE RELATED QUESTION: *What kind of pattern is used in this book?*
SAMPLE ACTIVITY: Engage students in important concepts (e.g., problem solving). Make hands-on materials accessible for students (number line, found materials). Encourage students to identify, describe, extend, and create repeating patterns using concrete materials and symbols for numeric patterning.

What Comes Next? by Kari Gold

SUMMARY: This big book begins with a key question, "Do you see a pattern here?" From the beginning, children engage in this interactive text. Opportunities to pose prompts and create an engaging rich dialog abound. Gold reinforces a strong real-world connection—both inside and outside the classroom.
CONNECTING STRANDS: Geometry and Spatial Sense, Measurement
READ AND DISCUSS: *What Comes Next?*
POSE RELATED QUESTION: *What do you think is going to happen next?*
SAMPLE ACTIVITY: Make available a variety of found and readymade materials. Have students explore and investigate the materials and make their own patterns. Invite them to share their unique patterns with their peers.

The Doorbell Rang by Pat Hutchins

SUMMARY: The children in the book are trying to divide a batch of cookies among themselves. As the story progresses, more and more friends arrive. They must continually figure out how many cookies each person gets.

CONNECTING STRANDS: Number Sense and Numeration, Data Management and Probability, Measurement

READ AND DISCUSS: *The Doorbell Rang*

POSE RELATED QUESTION: *What kind of pattern is used to create this story?*

SAMPLE ACTIVITY: Make linked cubes available to students. Have them use the linked cubes to uncover a pattern represented in the story. Students graph the data and write a rule to describe their pattern.

Patterns All Around Me by Trisha Jones

SUMMARY: A little girl sees patterns in nature all around her.

CONNECTING STRANDS: Number Sense and Numeration, Data Management and Probability

READ AND DISCUSS: *Patterns All Around Me*

POSE RELATED QUESTION: *Is there a pattern to the number of petals on a flower?*

SAMPLE ACTIVITY: Invite students to make a postcard drawing of something in nature that has a strong pattern.

Arithme-tickle: An Even Number of Odd Riddle Rhymes by Patrick Lewis

SUMMARY: Lewis uses rhyming text and illustrations to present a variety of math puzzles to solve. This book of riddles stimulates students to write their own riddles. Some riddles may contain a clue to be defined in order to solve the problem. Rhyming word problems inspire young problem-solvers to practice math strategies. An excellent book to enhance children's understanding of numerical and algebraic operations.

CONNECTING STRAND: Number Sense and Numeration

READ AND DISCUSS: *Arithme-tickle: An Even Number of Odd Riddle Rhymes*

POSE RELATED QUESTION: *What number puzzle can you create that is similar to the puzzles created in this book?*

SAMPLE ACTIVITY: Have students create their own math puzzles using word patterns. In partners, students exchange puzzles and work together to solve the problem. Encourage students to present their solutions orally.

A Pair of Socks by Stuart J. Murphy

SUMMARY: The premise of this short picture book is trying to figure out the difference between the pair of colorful socks. Murphy's rhyming text teaches patterns, early math skills, and problem-solving skills.

CONNECTING STRAND: Number Sense and Numeration

READ AND DISCUSS: *A Pair of Socks*

POSE RELATED QUESTION: *What other story can you make using another pair of items (e.g., mittens)?*

SAMPLE ACTIVITY: Have students use two of something and make their own pattern story. Have them share their stories with the larger group.

One Hundred Hungry Ants by Elinor J. Pinczes

SUMMARY: Pinczes describes how 100 ants arrange themselves in several rows of different sizes (e.g., 4 lines of 25) to get to the picnic faster. A problem arises. With all the rearranging, by the time the ants reach the picnic other animals have taken the food.

CONNECTING STRANDS: Geometry and Spatial Sense, Number Sense and Numeration
READ AND DISCUSS: *One Hundred Hungry Ants*
POSE RELATED QUESTION: *How many different ways are there to make 100?*
SAMPLE ACTIVITY: Have children use the Unifix Cubes to explore and investigate the number of different ways to make 100.

The Button Box by Margarette S. Reid

SUMMARY: A terrific book for encouraging sorting and classification leading to exploration and investigation of different kinds of patterning.
CONNECTING STRAND: Number Sense and Numeration
READ AND DISCUSS: *The Button Box*
POSE RELATED QUESTION: *What other materials could you sort to show your understanding of patterning?*
SAMPLE ACTIVITY: Have children bring in their own collections and make their own patterns.

Lots and Lots of Zebra Stripes by Stephen Swinburne

SUMMARY: An introduction to pattern recognition. The foreword discusses patterns and where they can be found in nature. Swinburne describes patterns in both general and specific terms. The last section poses questions designed to help children think about their own environment. This is a great springboard for discussions.
CONNECTING STRAND: Data Management and Probability
READ AND DISCUSS: *Lots and Lots of Zebra Stripes*
POSE RELATED QUESTION: *What other animal can you think of that has a strong pattern connection?*
SAMPLE ACTIVITY: Invite students to draw a picture of their animal and tell what they believe to be the purpose of the pattern. Have students make a class bar graph grouping the number of animals around a common purpose.

Math for All Seasons by Greg Tang

SUMMARY: Tang takes children on a journey to look for patterns, symmetries, and familiar number combinations. Each poem poses a "How many?" question about the accompanying seasonal items. Children are challenged to use patterns to solve problems in new and unexpected ways, as they look for patterns in order to add up the objects without counting one by one.
CONNECTING STRAND: Number Sense and Numeration
READ AND DISCUSS: *Math for All Seasons*
POSE RELATED QUESTION: *How do you use patterns to solve problems?*
SAMPLE ACTIVITY: Have students use patterns (words, pictures, and graphics) in their math journals to show how patterns are useful in solving problems.

Patterning and Algebra – Literature/Math Manipulative Organizer

MATHEMATICAL PROCESSES

Problem Solving; Reasoning and Proving; Reflecting; Selecting Tools and Computational Strategies; Connecting; Representing; Communicating

Title/ Author	Concepts/Skills/Topics/Additional Comments	Literary Style/Type	Math Manipulatives/Found Materials
Rooster's Off to See the World Eric Carle	Patterning–growing and declining patterns, repetitive text	Fiction–story	Found materials, number line, Unifix Cubes
The Very Hungry Caterpillar Eric Carle	Patterns–sequencing and growing, relations and functions	Fiction–story	Attribute blocks
Five Little Monkeys Jumping on the Bed Eileen Christelow	Patterning	Fiction–rhyming text	Found materials, pattern blocks, linked cubes
The House That Jack Built Elizabeth Falconer	Patterning–growing patterns	Fiction–story	Number line, linked cubes
Each Orange Had 8 Slices Paul Giganti	Number patterns, counting	Fiction–verse	Pattern blocks
Skip-Counting Kari Gold	Patterning–counting/growing patterns, addition, groupings–2s, 3s, 5s, real-world applications	Big book–rhyming text	Hundreds chart, abacus, number line
What Comes Next? Kari Gold	Patterning–growing patterns, real-world applications	Big book–inquiry	Coins, 3-D shapes
The Doorbell Rang Pat Hutchins	Patterning, growing patterns, tables and rules	Fiction–story, concept book	Hundreds chart, linked cubes
Patterns All Around Me Trisha Jones	Patterns in nature	Non-fiction	
Arithme-tickle Patrick Lewis	Algebraic operations, repeat patterns	Riddles–rhyming text	Pattern blocks
A Pair of Socks Stuart J. Murphy	Pattern recognition, matching, sorting, classifying, comparing	Story–rhyming text	Found materials
One Hundred Hungry Ants Elinor J. Pinczes	Patterning, tables and rules, rhyming text	Fiction–story	Hundreds chart
The Button Box Margarette S. Reid	Patterning, relationships, functions, sorting by size and function, real-world applications	Fiction–story	Hundreds chart, found materials, attribute blocks
Lots and Lots of Zebra Stripes Stephen Swinburne	Patterning–patterns in nature, repeated patterns; environmental connection, critical thinking, posing questions, real-world applications	Non-fiction–concept book	Household objects, nature–living things
Math for All Seasons Greg Tang	Reasoning, problem solving, real-world applications	Riddles–poetry	Pattern blocks

Sample Math-Related Manipulatives

Data Management and Probability

BIG IDEAS

Probability

Collection and Organization of Data

Data Relationships

Math-Related Literature Suggestions

Pigs at Odds: Fun with Math and Games Amy Axelrod	***Cloudy with a Chance of Meatballs*** Judi Barrett	***Country Fair*** Gail Gibbons	***No Fair*** Caren Holtzman	***The Great Graph Contest*** Loreen Leedy
Purple, Green and Yellow Robert Munsch	***Probably Pistachio*** Stuart J. Murphy	***The Best Vacation Ever*** Stuart J. Murphy	***Tally O'Malley*** Stuart J. Murphy	***Lemonade for Sale*** Stuart J. Murphy
Tiger Math: Learning to Graph from a Baby Tiger Ann Whitehead Nagda and Cindy Bickel	***Graph It*** Jennifer Osborne	***Caps for Sale*** Esphyr Slobokina	***Red Is Best*** Kathy Stinson	***Seven Blind Mice*** Ed Young

Data Management and Probability

Reflecting on the thinking patterns of this Grade 10 student around the notion of probability, reminds me where, when, and how young children begin to learn about probability. While students (Grade 3 and upwards) demonstrate a fundamental understanding of number, young children are just beginning the process. For example, on one occasion I took my grandsons to the fair. They saw a water-duck game they wanted to play. To win a prize, all they had to do was select one of the ducks and look at the number on the bottom of the duck. Anyone that played could win a small prize, but only a few lucky ones could win a large prize. What would the probability be of one or even two of the boys winning the large prize? Would it depend on how many had already won the large prize? Would it depend on the number of tries the boys took? Would the color of the duck they chose matter? Probability can be learned by everyone. Current research suggests children should study probability through lessons of experience, explore contexts, investigate, make predictions, and engage in probabilistic thinking through the use of hands-on models such as spinners, graphing mats, and dice.

Gaming, a popular sport for most children, provides opportunities for informal experiences in probability. The sophistication of these games, built on the idea of chance, challenges any young mind to discuss probabilistic situations with their family and peers on a consistent basis. "Ideas about probability (preK–2) should be informal and focus on judgments that children make because of their experiences." (*Principles and Standards for School Mathematics.*)

When not plugged into any number of game stations or engaged in old familiar games such as Chess, Snakes and Ladders, or Checkers, children can read children's books as good sources to develop their own games. "Activities should take the form of answering questions about the likelihood of events using vocabulary such as: more likely or less likely as opposed to asking children to view probability as numbers, calculations and ratios." (*Principles and Standards for School Mathematics.*)

The Data Management and Probability strand focuses on the development of these Big Ideas: Collecting Data and Conducting Surveys, Organizing Data, Constructing and Labelling Graphs, Investigating Simple Probability Situations, and Performing Simple Experiments. Collecting data and representing the data through graphic organizers such as the pictograph, bar graph, and line graph is all part of data analysis. Children's literature can promote young children's developing understanding of data management and probability. It's a great resource for introducing relevant vocabulary such as *fairness, chance, likely, unlikely,* and *impossible* to describe events. Pictographs, tallying and bar graphs, and vocabulary associated with data analysis can also be addressed using children's books. As teachers, we can create related activities that provide new hands-on experiences and help children understand the Big Ideas of Data Management and Probability.

Classroom Implementation – Preplanning

STRAND: Data Management and Probability
BIG IDEA: Constructing and Labelling Graphs
KEY CONCEPTS/SKILLS: Collecting information, counting and making tallies, surveying peers, sorting objects, making graphs, making observations from a graph

Big Idea Text Set – Linking Math Manipulatives and Math-Related Literature

Graphing

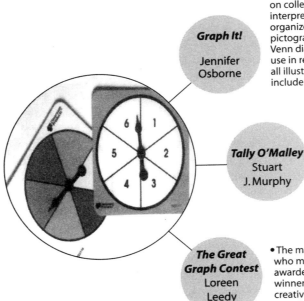

Graph It!
Jennifer Osborne

• This big book is filled with key information on collecting data, using tallying, and interpreting data using a variety of graphic organizers. Osborne introduces children to pictographs, bar graphs, circle graphs, and Venn diagrams. Measurement tools and their use in real-world contexts are embedded in all illustrations. This is an essential book to include in your collection.

Tally O'Malley
Stuart J. Murphy

• A very familiar storyline. The O'Malley family is off on a vacation. It will be a long ride. To keep busy, they play a game that most children play: they count all the gray cars or green T-shirts they see along the way and keep a tally of each. The person with the most tally marks wins the game. A good focus on the concept of tallying both in text and in use of visual graphics.

The Great Graph Contest
Loreen Leedy

• The main characters set up a contest to see who makes the best graph. Points are awarded based on predetermined criteria. A winner is declared based on correct math, creativity, and neatness. An excellent book to introduce data analysis from data collection (tallies and surveys) to the use of organizers (Venn diagrams, quantity graphs, circle graphs, picture graphs, and bar graphs). Leedy carefully outlines the process for data collection and contruction.

Problem: Question related to the underpinning concepts in the selected text.
Instructional Approach: Independent Math—Math Discovery Hubs

Classroom Example in Action

LEAD BOOK: *The Great Graph Contest*
READ AND DISCUSS: In a large group, read and discuss the story *The Great Graph Contest.*
ENGAGE: Provide opportunities for students to engage in the text. Read aloud the companion concept book *Graph It!* Pose questions in reference to the text and graphic organizers: *Which column…? How many…?*
POSE RELATED QUESTION: *What is the purpose of graphic organizers? Can you think of a situation where you would need to use a graphic organizer? Explain.*

Data Management and Probability Discovery Hub

Graphing

MATH CENTRE 1 — Activity
- **Materials:** Display five different electronic games that are familiar to students. Rule up a tally sheet using the five game pictures.
- Ask students to walk around the room, ask their friends which game they prefer, and put a tally mark in the right column.
- Have them count the number of tally marks in each column.
- Share with the larger group.

MATH CENTRE 2 — Activity
- **Materials:** colored plastic tablecloth, variety of fruits
- Review *Graph It!*
- Use the pictograph format and write the catagories of fruits for the column headings.
- Cover a classroom table.
- Focus on constructing a cooperative class pictograph using the fruits.
- Have students use their math journals to create their own pictographs.

MATH CENTRE 3 — Activity
- **Materials:** graphing mats
- Have students bring in their personal collections (shells, rocks, etc.).
- Review the bar graph.
- Construct a bar graph using the objects from their own collections.
- Share with the larger group.

MATH CENTRE 4 — Activity
- **Materials:** a wide variety of materials
- Read *The Great Graph Contest.*
- Plan a class contest.
- In small groups, students create their own graph and submit it to the contest.
- Allow time for presenting the graphs and for peer comment.

OTHER PATTERNING BOOK SUGGESTIONS

Carle, Eric. *The Grouchy Ladybug.*
Hoberman, Mary Ann. *A House Is a House for Me.*
Jonas, Ann. *Round Trip.*
Pluckrose, Henry. *Math Counts: Sorting.*

Linking Math Centre Activities and Assessment Strategies

Activity	Observation	Interview/Conference	Portfolio	Self/Peer	Performance	Math Journal	Rubric	Checklist
1	✔							
2						✔		
3		✔						
4					✔			

Recommended Books, Sample Activities, and a Suggested Process for Implementing the Management and Probability Strand

Pigs at Odds: Fun with Math and Games by Amy Axelrod

SUMMARY: The Pigs are raring to go to the country fair to play games and win prizes. No matter how many times Mr. Pig tries to win, however, the odds seem to be against him. This book provides a wonderful opportunity to discuss math language related to probability (e.g., *chance, fair, likelihood, unlikelihood*). At the end of the book, Axelrod provides an explanation of odds and probability and what makes a game fair.

CONNECTING STRAND: Number Sense and Numeration

READ AND DISCUSS: *Pigs at Odds: Fun with Math and Games*

POSE RELATED QUESTION: *What is the likelihood that Mr. Pig will go home a winner?*

SAMPLE ACTIVITY: In small groups, have students refer to *Pigs at Odds*. Invite them to create a picture and word list of vocabulary related to probability. Use the book to help provide meaningful understandings.

Cloudy with a Chance of Meatballs by Judi Barrett

SUMMARY: What is the likelihood of rain tomorrow? A tall tale with a take on the weather told with a lot of humor and imagination. For example, how many times have you heard about a town that rains *food?* This book is a good springboard to discussing the likelihood or unlikelihood or predicting the weather. Great real-world connection.

CONNECTING STRAND: Measurement

READ AND DISCUSS: *Cloudy with a Chance of Meatballs*

POSE RELATED QUESTION: *What is the likelihood that it will rain tomorrow?*

SAMPLE ACTIVITY: In small groups, have students create a probability game using spinners. Have students write the rules to the game and present the game to the class.

Country Fair by Gail Gibbons

SUMMARY: A fact-filled picture book describing what one is likely to find at a New England country fair. Brightly colored illustrations of animals, people, and objects fill each page.

CONNECTING STRAND: Number Sense and Numeration

READ AND DISCUSS: *Country Fair*

POSE RELATED QUESTION: *What way can you show others what you observed at the fair?*

SAMPLE ACTIVITY: In a large group, review the book *Country Fair* with the students. Ask students to make a tally of the number of animals seen at the fair. Have them create a bar graph to show their sightings. Tell students: *Be sure to include important headings on your bar graph.*

No Fair! by Caren Holtzman

SUMMARY: Probability as it relates to fairness is addressed in the context of children playing familiar games of checkers, jacks, marbles, and dice. In playing the games, issues of equity come to the forefront. Who gets to choose the game? Do both have an equal shot at winning checkers if a piece is missing?

CONNECTING STRAND: Number Sense and Numeration

READ AND DISCUSS: *No Fair!*

POSE RELATED QUESTION: *How would you design a fair game?*

SAMPLE ACTIVITY: Make available a copy of *Probability Games and Other Activities* by Ivan Moscovich. Have students play the games and select the concrete materials (spinners, dice, playing cards, etc.) to create a "fair" game.

The Great Graph Contest by Loreen Leedy

SUMMARY: In this story, the main characters set up a contest to see who makes th[...]
graph. Points are awarded based on predetermined criteria. A winner is declared ba[...]
on correct math, creativity, and neatness. An excellent book to introduce data analysis
from data collection (tallies and surveys) to the use of graphic organizers (Venn diagrams, quantity graphs, circle graphs, picture graphs, and bar graphs). Leedy carefully
outlines the process for data collection and construction.

CONNECTING STRAND: Number Sense and Numeration

READ AND DISCUSS: *The Great Graph Contest*

POSE RELATED QUESTION: *Was there value in having a contest to learn about how to organize information accurately? Explain.*

SAMPLE ACTIVITY: In pairs, students create their own graph modelling the scenario
from the book. Have students use the same criteria to judge the completed graphs.
Engage students in self- and peer evaluation.

Purple, Green and Yellow by Robert Munsch

SUMMARY: The story begins with a young child's desire to have markers like those of her
friends. What happens next reminds me of a familiar situation that happens all the time
in the real world. Opportunities to introduce children to gathering data, tallying the data,
and representing the data using an organizer abound.

CONNECTING STRANDS: Number Sense and Numeration

READ AND DISCUSS: *Purple, Green and Yellow*

POSE RELATED QUESTION: *How can you show the number of purple, green, and yellow
markers used by your classmates?*

SAMPLE ACTIVITY: Have students take a class survey of the colors purple, green, and yellow. Have students tally the results. What is the class's favorite color? Invite students to
make a pictograph to represent the class results.

Probably Pistachio by Stuart J. Murphy

SUMMARY: Analyzing data and making predictions are at the core of successful decision-making. During the course of one terrible day, Jack learns all about probability
terms such as *possible, likely,* and *certain.* Jack assesses his chances of his day improving,
guessing what the outcomes of each activity will be. At the back, Murphy suggests games
and ideas for continued practice.

CONNECTING STRAND: Number Sense and Numeration

READ AND DISCUSS: *Probably Pistachio*

POSE RELATED QUESTION: *How many doubled-sided counters will fall on the red side?
How many on the yellow?*

SAMPLE ACTIVITY: Make double-sided counters available. Have students make predictions as to how many counters will fall on the red side and how many on the yellow side.

The Best Vacation Ever by Stuart J. Murphy

SUMMARY: Where will the family go for their vacation? To answer the question, one
family member takes a survey of everyone's destination preferences and gathers the data.
Murphy includes examples of the charts used to organize the data, providing a good
example for students in gathering data. Although the book stops short of discussing how
the information should be interpreted, it works nicely in springboarding to a future
discussion on interpreting the data.

CONNECTING STRANDS: Number Sense and Numeration

READ AND DISCUSS: *The Best Vacation Ever*

POSE RELATED QUESTION: *Is there a tool you can use to display your information in a different way? How?*

SAMPLE ACTIVITY: Have students use the tallied data from the story. Invite them to select a graphic organizer and create a graph to represent the data.

Tally O'Malley by Stuart J. Murphy

SUMMARY: A very familiar storyline. The math concept is tallying. The O'Malleys are off on vacation but getting there will be a long drive. To keep busy, they play tally games—counting all the gray cars or green T-shirts they see. The person with the most tally marks wins.

CONNECTING STRAND: Number Sense and Numeration

READ AND DISCUSS: *Tally O'Malley*

POSE RELATED QUESTION: *In what other situation would tallying be useful? Explain.*

SAMPLE ACTIVITY: Challenge students to think of another situation to practice tallying. Have them present their scenarios orally, and display their work in the classroom.

Lemonade for Sale by Stuart J. Murphy

SUMMARY: A wonderful book for introducing bar graphs. It combines kids selling lemonade and the use of graphs and marketing in a creative narrative.

CONNECTING STRAND: Number Sense and Numeration

READ AND DISCUSS: *Lemonade for Sale*

POSE QUESTION: *Review the story* Lemonade for Sale. *Would a bar graph be useful if you were selling another product?*

SAMPLE ACTIVITY: Have students choose their own product and make a bar graph using the story as a pattern to follow in marketing their product.

Tiger Math: Learning to Graph from a Baby Tiger by Ann Whitehead Nagda and Cindy Bickel

SUMMARY: This is the true story of a baby tiger whose mother dies when it is very young. The story is told as a narrative and uses all sorts of graphic organizers (picture graphs, bar graphs, circle graphs, line graphs) to help children understand ideas ranging from number of species alive to different types of species. The authors show the functional use of graphs in making comparisons and predictions while stressing interpreting data.

CONNECTING STRAND: Number Sense and Numeration

READ AND DISCUSS: *Tiger Math: Learning to Graph from a Baby Tiger*

POSE RELATED QUESTION: *Are there different functional uses for specific graphs?*

SAMPLE ACTIVITY: Have students review *Tiger Math*. Ask them to think of a situation where making a graph would be a good way to present information. Ask them: *What graphic organizer is most suitable to represent your information? Draw the type of graph you selected and write about its suitability and use in your math journal.*

Graph It! by Jennifer Osborne

SUMMARY: This big book is filled with key information on collecting data, using tallying, and interpreting data using a variety of graphic organizers. Children explore pictographs, bar graphs, line graphs, circle graphs, and Venn diagrams. Osborne embeds measurement tools and their use in real-world contexts in the illustrations. This is an essential book to include in your collection.

CONNECTING STRANDS: Measurement, Number Sense and Numeration

READ AND DISCUSS: *Graph It!*

POSE RELATED QUESTION: *Is there a special purpose for each specific graphic organizer?*

SAMPLE ACTIVITY: Instruct students: *Choose a graph to display new information. Search newspapers to find two examples of the graphic organizer you selected. Paste the examples in your math journal and explain the use of this model and its real-life application.*

Caps for Sale by Esphyr Slobodkina

SUMMARY: This is the story of a peddler who sells caps. Instead of carrying his wares on his back, he wears them on his head. One morning, he goes for a walk and falls asleep under a tree, the caps piled high on his head. When he wakes, he finds monkeys in a tree have taken them. While trying many ways to get his caps back, he notices the monkeys have copied his actions. When he throws his cap on the ground, they follow. The peddler quickly gathers up his caps.

CONNECTING STRANDS: Number Sense and Numeration, Patterning and Algebra

READ AND DISCUSS: *Caps for Sale*

POSE RELATED QUESTION: *Was there a popular color in the cap collection? Explain.*

SAMPLE ACTIVITY: Have students make a tally chart to reflect the number of different-colored caps. Then, have students make a pictograph representing the peddler's cap collection.

Red Is Best by Kathy Stinson

SUMMARY: This the story of a little girl, Kelly, whose favorite color is red. Kelly's mother tries to convince her to wear something other than red.

CONNECTING STRAND: Patterning and Algebra

READ AND DISCUSS: *Red Is Best*

POSE RELATED QUESTION: *What is the likelihood that Kelly will wear red the next day?*

SAMPLE ACTIVITY: Make spinners available to students. Invite them to predict how many spins it will take for the spinner to land on red. Have students make a T-chart to record the number of spins predicted and the number of actual spins it took to stop on red.

Seven Blind Mice by Ed Young

SUMMARY: This book retells the ancient Buddhist tale of seven blind mice who try to decide what an elephant is like based on examining one part of it. Six of them draw incorrect conclusions based on one feel. The seventh mouse takes its time and learns the truth about the elephant. The book reinforces the importance of collecting all data before drawing conclusions—a vital message to instill in students. An offshoot is a connection to the Patterning and Algebra strand. For example, the mice are each of a different color and examine the elephant on a different day of the week. The moral of the story is: If you work together as a team, you can accomplish any task. But alone, you cannot.

CONNECTING STRANDS: Patterning and Algebra, Number Sense and Numeration

READ AND DISCUSS: *Seven Blind Mice*

POSE RELATED QUESTION: *What is the probability that one of the mice could solve the problem?*

SAMPLE ACTIVITY: Have students use various virtual manipulatives to perform probability experiments.

Data Management and Probability – Literature/Math Manipulative Organizer

MATHEMATICAL PROCESSES

Problem Solving; Reasoning and Proving; Reflecting; Selecting Tools and Computational Strategies; Connecting; Representing; Communicating

Title/Author	Concepts/Skills/Topics/Additional Comments	Literary Style/Type	Math Manipulatives/Found Materials
Pigs at Odds Amy Axelrod	Probability–chance, idea of fairness, math language: likelihood/ unlikelihood	Fiction–picture book	Concrete materials
Cloudy with a Chance of Meat-balls Judi Barrett	Data analysis, probability, graphing, collecting data, predicting	Fiction–comic book format, fantasy	Spinners, dice
Country Fair Gail Gibbons	Data collection, sorting, classifying, organizing	Fiction–picture book	Graphing materials–grid paper/chart paper
No Fair! Caren Holtzman	Idea of fairness, chance, experimental–probability, real-life connections	Non-fiction–play format	Spinners, dice, playing cards
The Great Graph Contest Loreen Leedy	Surveys, tallies, variety of graphs–circle, Venn diagram, picture, bar; cartoon illustrations	Fiction	Graphing materials–grid paper/chart paper
Purple, Green and Yellow Robert Munsch	Data analysis, graphing, tallying, data collection, sorting, classifying, organizing	Fiction	Graphing materials–grid paper/chart paper
Probably Pistachio Stuart J. Murphy	Data analysis, probability– chance, prediction, likelihood	Fiction	Double-sided counters
The Best Vacation Ever Stuart J. Murphy	Data collection–sorting, classifying, organizing, charting	Fiction	Graphing materials–grid paper/chart paper
Tally O'Malley Stuart J. Murphy	Addition, surveying, tallying	Fiction	Graphing materials
Lemonade for Sale Stuart J. Murphy	Bar graphs	Fiction	Graphing materials
Tiger Math Ann Whitehead Nagda, Cindy Bickel	Functional use of graphs, graphic organizers–bar, circle, line. Skills: comparing, predicting, interpreting	Non-fiction–narrative	Graphing materials
Graph It! Jennifer Osborne	Graphic organizers–pictograph, circle, bar, Venn diagram; measurement, real-life applications	Information–concept book	Graphing materials and other concrete materials
Caps for Sale Esphyr Slobodkina	Tallying, graphing	Fiction–big book	Graphing materials
Red Is Best Kathy Stinson	Probability–likelihood/ unlikelihood	Fiction–story	Chart paper/stickers, dice, spinners
Seven Blind Mice Ed Young	Probability	Fiction–fable, poetic text	Virtual manipulatives

A Final Note

Participating in our classroom marble-structure activity provided some firsthand experience in classroom integration. As we worked through the project, we infused our math knowledge (problem solving), science background (structures), and language skills (oral communication) in order to complete the task. This practice proved effective, as each group ultimately achieved the stated expectations. The practice also modelled how math, science, and language skills naturally infuse to create learning environments. Infusing subjects to teach lessons is not only efficient, it can help teachers guide students through curriculum and advance their higher-order thinking skills, thereby improving their overall academic performance.

—Reflections of a prospective teacher

Throughout *Math Memories You Can Count On*, I have suggested engaging children's literature as a springboard for developing meaningful mathematical understandings within and across all five mathematics strands.

"Text sets," a term first introduced by Carolyn Burke, provide a starting point for integrating math and literature. I have identified the connecting strands for each book for future planning, to facilitate strong linkages between numeracy and literacy skills and concepts.

I have included a number of organizers in each strand to serve as models for planning future literature-based math lessons. The beginning organizer for each strand opens with the Big Ideas and provides a list of 15 Math-Related Literature suggestions. As you uncover fiction and non-fiction math-related books that address the Big Ideas, you may want to personalize your own planning. To assist you in planning, the graphic organizers in Appendix C make up a blank template for future use.

An integral component of the literature-based math strategy is the use of math manipulatives. The Big Idea Text Set Organizer for each strand demonstrates the literature and math manipulative connections. You may want to pre-plan using this type of organizer to reinforce the importance of using hands-on math manipulatives to ensure greater understanding of math concepts. Appendix C supplies a reproducible template to assist you on page 115.

Other blank templates will help in the planning process:

- Math Discovery Hub, which will help you plan the hands-on learning centres that support the Big Ideas (page 117)
- Linking Math Centre Activities and Assessment Strategies template (page 119)
- Literature/Math Manipulative Organizer template (page 121)

As students identify relationships between math concepts and everyday situations and make connections between math and other subject areas, they develop the ability and confidence to use math to extend and apply their knowledge in other curriculum areas.

—The newly revised Ontario *Math Curriculum* document.

As the prospective teacher has reflected, stories can also act as a bridge between mathematics and other curricular areas. Encourage children to make interdisciplinary connections during a brainstorming session. Use these connections to integrate different subject areas. Using children's literature in the mathematics classroom encourages lifelong learning through real-world connections that will lead to positive math memories for all students.

Acknowledgements

I am grateful to my friend and colleague Mary for sharing her math memories. Her memories became the catalyst for the title of this book, *Math Memories You Can Count On*.

A great big thank-you to all prospective and experienced teachers who were willing to share their "real" math memories and math reflections throughout this book. Collectively they provided insight into their attitudes, beliefs, and predispositions about how mathematics was taught. Through their insight, we learn how and what kind of mathematics should be taught to encourage positive beliefs and attitudes in students of today's primary classrooms.

A special thanks to Scholastic Canada for their continuing support and encouragement in providing much-needed print resources. To Spectrum Educational Supplies for providing me with the math manipulatives. To Judy Halpern of the Magic Suitcase for sharing some of her best mathematics children's literature. To my friend and colleague Dr. George Gadanidis, whose ongoing research in the field has encouraged many teachers to see the "beauty and music" of mathematics. Thanks also to my hardworking editor, Alan Simpson, whose skillful suggestions have made this book an excellent resource for teaching elementary mathematics. And finally, to my husband, Maurice, for helping me overcome many of the technology-related glitches I encountered throughout the writing of this book.

In writing this book, I hope to encourage teachers of primary classrooms to link children's literature and mathematics for effective teaching and learning of mathematics.

Appendix A Children's Literature

Adler, David A., and Nancy Tobin. 1998. *How Tall, How Short, How Faraway?* Holiday House.

Adler, David A., and Nancy Tobin. 1998. *Shape Up! Fun with Triangles and other Polygons.* Holiday House.

Aker, Suzanne, and Bernie Karlin. 1993. *What Comes in 2's,3's & 4's?* Scholastic.

Allen, Pamela. 1990. *Who Sank the Boat?* Puffin.

Anno, Masaichiro. 1983. *Anno's Mysterious Multiplying Jar.* Penguin.

Axelrod, Amy, and Sharon McGinley-Nally. 2003. *Pigs at Odds: Fun with Math and Games.* Aladdin.

Axelrod, Amy, and Sharon McGinley-Nally. 1999. *Pigs in the Pantry: Fun with Math and Cooking.* Aladdin.

Axelrod, Amy, and Sharon McGinley-Nally. 1997. *Pigs Will Be Pigs: Fun with Math and Money.* Aladdin.

Barrett, Judy, et al. 1978. *Cloudy with a Chance of Meatballs.* (cassette tape with paperback book) Live Oak Media.

Base, Graeme. 2006. *Uno's Garden.* Harry N. Abrams.

Brisson, Pat. 1993. *Benny's Pennies.* Doubleday.

Brown, Anne, and Jaime Zollars. 2006. *The Great Math Tattle Battle.* Albert Whitman.

Burns, Marilyn, and Martha Weston. 1978. *The Book About Time.* Little Brown.

Burns, Marilyn, and Gordon Silveria. 2008. *The Greedy Triangle.* Scholastic.

Burns, Marilyn, and Debbie Tilley. 2008. *Spaghetti and Meatballs For All.* Scholastic.

Burns, Marilyn, and Martha Weston. 1978. *This Book Is About Time.* Little Brown.

Callella-Jones, Trisha, et al.1998. *Patterns All Around Me.* Creative Teaching.

Carle, Eric. 2002. *Draw Me a Star.* Puffin.

Carle, Eric. 1996. *The Grouchy Ladybug.* HarperCollins.

Carle, Eric. 1991. *Rooster's Off to See the World.* Simon & Schuster.

Carle, Eric. 1969. *The Very Hungry Caterpillar.* Philomel.

Christelow, Eileen. 2008. *Five Little Monkeys Jumping on the Bed.* Sandpiper.

Clements, Andrew, and Mike Reed. 2006. *A Million Dots.* Simon & Schuster.

Clement, Rod. 1999. *Counting on Frank.* Gareth Stevens.

Cuyler, Margery, and Arthur Howard. 2005. *100th Day Worries.* Aladdin.

Dobson, Christine, and Matthew Holmes. 2003. *Pizza Counting.* Topeka Bindery.

Dodds, Dayle Ann, and Julie Lacome. 1996. *The Shape of Things.* Topeka Bindery.

Emberley, Ed. 1988. *The Wing on a Flea: A Book About Shapes.* Little Brown.

Falconer, Elizabeth. 1994. *The House That Jack Built.* Ideal Children's Books.

Franco, Betsy, and Steve Jenkins. 2008. *Bees, Snails, & Peacock Tails: Patterns & Shapes… Naturally.* Margaret K. McElderry.

Friedman, Aileen. 1995. *A Cloak for the Dreamer.* Scholastic.

Friedman, Aileen, and Susan Guevara. 1995. *The King's Commissioners.* Scholastic.

Gag, Wanda. 2006. *Millions of Cats.* Puffin.

Garland, Michael. 2007. *How Many Mice?* Dutton.

Gerth, Melanie, and Laura Huliska-Beith. 2000. *Ten Little Ladybugs.* Piggy Toes.

Gibbons, Gail. 1994. *Country Fair.* Little Brown.

Giganti, Paul. 1992. *Each Orange Had 8 Slices.* Greenwillow.

Gleick, Beth, and Marthe Jocelyn. 2008. *Time Is When.* Tundra.

Gold, Kari Jenson. 1999. *It's Time!* Scholastic.

Gold, Kari Jenson. 1996. *3-D Figures.* Scholastic.

Gold, Kari Jenson. 1996. *Numbers Every Day.* Scholastic.

Gold, Kari Jenson. 1999, *Parts of a Whole.* Scholastic.

Gold, Kari Jenson. 2002. *Short, Tall, Big, or Small?* Scholastic.

Gold, Kari Jenson. 2002. *Let's Skip-Count.* Scholastic.

Gold, Kari Jenson. 1998. *What Comes Next?* Scholastic.

Goldstone, Bruce. 2006. *Great Estimations.* Henry Holt.

Greene, Rhonda Gowler, and James Kaczman. 1997. *When a Line Bends… A Shape Begins.* Houghton Mifflin.

Hamm, Diane Johnston. 1994. *How Many Feet in the Bed?* Aladdin.

Hightower, Susan, and Matt Novak. 1997. *Twelve Snails to One Lizard: A Tale of Mischief and Measurement.* Simon & Schuster.

Hoban, Tana. 2000. *Cubes, Cones, Cylinders & Spheres.* HarperCollins.

Hoban, Tana. 1985. *Is It Larger? Is It Smaller?* William Morrow.

Hoban, Tana. 1987. *Is it Red? Is it Yellow? Is it Blue?* HarperCollins.

Hoberman, Mary Ann, et al. 1982. *A House Is a House for Me.* (cassette tape with paperback book) Live Oak Media.

Holtzman, Caren. 1995. *A Quarter from the Tooth Fairy.* Scholastic.

Holtzman, Caren. 1997. *No Fair.* Cartwheel.

Holub, Joan. 2003. *Riddle-iculous Math.* Albert Whitman.

Hutchins, Pat. 1989. *The Doorbell Rang.* Greenwillow .

Hutchins, Pat. 1987. *Changes, Changes.* Aladdin.

Hutchins, Pat. 1994. *Clocks and More Clocks.* Aladdin.

Hutchins, Hazel. 2004. *A Second Is a Hiccup.* Scholastic.

Jonas, Ann. 1984. *The Quilt.* HarperCollins.

Jonas, Ann. 1990. *Round Trip.* Greenwillow.

Leedy, Loreen. 1992. *Monster Money Book.* Holiday House.

Leedy, Loreen. 1994. *Fraction Action.* Holiday House.

Leedy, Loreen. 2006. *The Great Graph Contest.* Holiday House.

Leedy, Loreen. 2000. *Subtraction Action.* Holiday House.

Lewis, Patrick. 2007. *Arithme-tickle: An Even Number of Odd Riddle-Rhymes.* Harcourt.

Ling, Bettina, and Michael Rex 1997. *The Fattest Tallest Snowman Ever.* Cartwheel.

LoPresti, Angeline Sparagna. 2003. *A Place for Zero.* Charlesbridge.

McNamara, Margaret, and G. Brian Karas. 2007. *How Many Seeds in a Pumpkin?* Schwartz & Wade.

Maccarone, Grace, and David Neuhaus. 1998. *Three Pigs, One Wolf and Seven Magic Shapes.* Scholastic.

Maestro, Betsy, et al. 2000. *The Story of Clocks and Calendars: Marking a Millennium.* HarperCollins.

Merriam Eve. 1996. *12 Ways to get to 11.* Aladdin.

Micklethwait, Lucy. 2004. *I Spy shapes in Art.* HarperCollins.

Munsch, Robert. 1995. *Moira's Birthday.* Annick.

Munsch, Robert, and Helene Desputeaux. 2007. *Purple, Green & Yellow.* Annikins.

Murphy, Stuart J., and Nadine Bernard Westcott. 1997. *The Best Vacation Ever.* HarperCollins.

Murphy, Stuart J., and Tricia Tusa. 1997. *Lemonade for Sale.* HarperCollins.

Murphy, Stuart J., et al. 1997. *Betcha: Estimating.* HarperCollins.

Murphy, Stuart J. 1996. *Give Me Half.* HarperCollins.

Murphy, Stuart J., and Frank Remkiewicz. 2003. *Less Than Zero.* HarperCollins.

Murphy, Stuart J. 2000. *A Pair of Socks: Matching.* HarperCollins.

Murphy, Stuart J., and Marsha Winborn. 2001. *Probably Pistachio.* HarperCollins.

Murphy, Stuart J. 2004. *Tally O'Malley.* Harper Trophy.

Murphy, Stuart, and Brian Floca. 2000. *Let's Fly a Kite.* HarperCollins.

Myllar, Rolf. 1991. *How Big is a Foot?* Yearling.

Nagda, Ann, and Cindy Bickel. 2002. *Tiger Math: Learning to Graph From a Baby Tiger.* Books for Young People.

Nayer, Judy. 1996. *How Many?* Newbridge Educational.

Nayer, Judy, et al, 1997. *More or Less?* Doubleday.

Nayer, Judy. 1996. *Up, Down, All Around.* Newbridge Educational.

Nayer, Judy. 1999. *What's the Shape?* Newbridge Educational.

Neuschwander, Cindy. 1988. *Amanda Bean's Amazing Dream.* Charlesbridge.

Neuschwander, Cindy. 2003. *Sir Cumference and the Sword in the Cone, a Math Adventure.* Charlesbridge.

Older, Jules, and Megan Halsey. 2002. *Telling Time.* Charlesbridge.

Osborne, Jennifer E. 1996. *Measuring Up!* Newbridge.

Osborne, Jennifer E. 1996. *Solve It!* Newbridge.

Osborne, Jennifer E. 1996. *Units of Measure.* Newbridge.

Pallotta, Jerry. 2003. *Count to a Million: 1,000,000.* Scholastic.

Patilla, Peter. 1999. *Sorting.* Heinemann.

Pinczes, Elinor J., and Bonnie MacKain. 2002. *A Remainder of One.* Sandpiper.

Pinczes, Elinor J., and Bonnie MacKain. 1999. *One Hundred Hungry Ants.* Sandpiper.

Pluckrose, Henry. 2001. *Math Counts: Sorting.* Children's Press.

Reid, Margarette, and Sarah Chamberlain. 1995. *The Button Box.* Puffin.

Schlein, Miriam, and Donald Crews. 1996. *More Than One.* HarperCollins.

Schwartz, David, and Steven Kellogg. 1989. *If You Made a Million.* HarperCollins.

Schwartz, David, and Steven Kellogg. 2006. *Millions to Measure.* HarperCollins.

Scieszka, Jon, and Lane Smith. 1995. *The Math Curse.* Viking.

Sierra, Judy. 2001. *Counting Crocodiles.* Harcourt.

Slobodkina, Esphyr. 1947. *Caps for Sale.* HarperCollins.

Stinson, Kathy, and Robin Baird Lewis. 2006. *Red is Best.* Annick.

Swinburne, Stephen. 1998. *Lots and Lots of Zebra Stripes: Patterns in Nature*. Boyd Mills.

Tang, Greg, and Harry Briggs. 2002. *The Best of Times*. Scholastic.

Tang, Greg, and Harry Briggs. 2004. *The Grapes of Math*. Scholastic.

Tang, Greg, and Harry Briggs. 2003. *Math Appeal*. Scholastic.

Tang, Greg, and Greg Paprocki. 2003. *MATH-terpieces*. Scholastic.

Tang, Greg, and Harry Briggs. 2005. *Math for All Seasons*. Scholastic.

Tang, Greg, and Harry Briggs. 2005. *Math Potatoes*. Scholastic.

Thong, Roseanne. 2000.*Round Is a Mooncake: A Book of Shapes*. Chronicle.

Tompert, Ann. 1990. *Grandfather Tang's Story*. Knopf.

Trumbauer, Lisa. 2005. *Graph It!* Compass Point.

Van Dusen, Chris. 2005. *If I Built a Car*. Puffin.

Wells, Robert E. 2000. *Can You Count to a Googol?* Topeka Bindery.

Wells, Robert E. 2005. *Is A Blue Whale the Biggest Thing There Is?* Franklin Watts.

Weston, Carrie, and Sophie Fatus. 2007. *If a Chicken Stayed for Supper*. Holiday House.

Williams, Sue. 2002. *Dinnertime!* Harcourt.

Young, Ed. 2002. *Seven Blind Mice*. Puffin.

Ziefert, Harriet. 2006. *You Can't Buy a Dinosaur with a Dime: Problem-Solving in Dollars and Cents*. Handprint Books/Ragged Bears/Blue Apple.

Appendix B Professional Literature

(*By order of appearance* in *Math Memories You Can Count On.*)

Preface

Early Math Strategy, The Report of the Expert Panel on Early Math in Ontario, 2003: p. 24.

Whitin, David, and Cassandra Gary. March 1994. *"Promoting Mathematical Explorations Through Children's Literature." Arithmetic Teacher.* v41 (n7): pp. 394–99.

Early Math Strategy Report, 1999: p. 9.

Whitin, David. May 2002. "The Potentials and Pitfalls of Integrating Literature into the Mathematics Program." *Teaching Children Mathematics.*

Friederwitzer, Fredda, and Barbara Berman. December 1999. "The Language of Time." *Teaching Children Mathematics:* pp. 254–59.

Chapter 1

Presto, Kevin, and Corey Drake. Dec. 2004/Jan. 2005. *Teaching Children Mathematics.*

McDuffie, Amy. 2004. "Mathematics Teaching as a Deliberate Practice: An Investigation of Elementary Pre-service Teachers' Reflective Thinking During Student Teaching." *Journal of Mathematics Teacher Education:* pp. 31–61.

Early Math Strategy, The Report of the Expert Panel on Early Math in Ontario, 2003.

Hellwig, S.J., E.E. Monroe, and J.S. Jacobs. 2000. "Making Informed Choices: Selecting Children's Trade Books for Mathematics Instruction." *Teaching Children Mathematics.*

Guillaume, Andrea, and Lisa Kirtman. February 2005. "Learning Lessons about Lessons: Memories of Mathematics Instruction." *Teaching Children Mathematics:* pp. 302–09.

Ball, Deborah, Sarah Lubienski, and Denise Mewborn. 2001. "Research on Teaching Mathematics: The Unsolved Problem of Teachers' Mathematical Knowledge." *Mathematics, A Handbook of Research on Teaching,* 4th ed. Washington D.C. American Association.

NCTM News Bulletin, Jan./Feb. 2008.

MCCain, M.F., and F. Mustard. 1999. *Early Years Study.*

Kamii, Constance. 2000. *First Graders Dividing 62 by 5: A Teacher Uses Piaget's Theory.*

Chapter 2

Trafton, Paul, and Carol Midgett. May 2001. "Learning Through Problems: A Powerful Approach to Teaching Mathematics." *Teaching Children Mathematics*: p. 532.

Facilitator's Handbook: A Guide to Effective Instruction in Mathematics, K–6. Teaching and Learning through Problem Solving. The Literacy and Numeracy Secretariat Professional Learning Series.

Ritchhart, Ron. April 1999. "Generative Topics: Building a Curriculum Around Big Ideas." *Teaching Children Mathematics*.

Principles and Standards for School Mathematics. NCTM, 2000.

Ball, Deborah. 1993. "Halves, Pieces and Twoths: Constructing Representational Contexts in Teaching Fractions." *Teaching Children Mathematics*: pp. 157–96.

Burns, Marilyn. 1992. *About Teaching Mathematics*: p. 1.

Carpenter, Thomas, et al. 1999. *Children's Mathematics: Cognitively Guided Instruction.*

Principles and Standards for School Mathematics NCTM, 1998.

The Ontario Curriculum: K–8.

Children and Mathematics. NCTM, 2000: p. 66.

Whitin, Phyllis, and David Whitin. 2000, "Promoting Communication in the Mathematics Classroom." *Children and Mathematics.* NCTM: p. 60.

Hunsader, Pat. 2004. "Mathematics Trade Books: Establishing Their Value and Assessing Their Quality." *The Reading Teacher.* 57: p. 618.

Moyer, Patricia, Johanna Bolyard, and Mark Spikell. Feb. 2003. "What Are Virtual Manipulatives?" *Teaching Children Mathematics.*

Chapter 3

A Guide to Effective Instruction in Mathematics, 2006.

Lewis, Barbara, Long, Roberta and Martha MacKay. April 1993. "Fostering Communication in Mathematics Using Children's Literature." *Arithmetic Teacher.*

Sherrill, Carl. March 2005. "Math Riddles: Helping Children Connect Words and Numbers." *Teaching Children Mathematics.* NCTM.

Chapter 4

Twain, Mark. 1884. *The Adventures of Huckleberry Finn.*

Huck, Charlotte, Susan Hepler, and Janet Hickman. 1987. *Children's Literature in the Elementary School.*

Reson, V.A. *Principles and Standards for School Mathematics.* NCTM, 2000.

Ducolon, Colin. March 2000. "Quality Literature as a Springboard to Problem Solving." *Teaching Children Mathematics.*

Facilitator's Handbook: A Guide to Effective Instruction in Mathematics, K–6. Teaching and Learning through Problem Solving. The Literacy and Numeracy Secretariat Professional Learning Series.

Chapter 5

Clements, D.H., and S. McMillen. 2002. "Rethinking 'Concrete' Manipulatives. In D. L. Chambers (Ed.), *Putting Research into Practice in the Elementary Grades.* NCTM: pp. 252–63.

Early Math Strategy, The Report of the Expert Panel on Early Math in Ontario, 2003: p. 27.

Heuser, Daniel. January 2000. "Math Class Becomes Learner Centred." *Teaching Children Mathematics.* NCTM: pp. 288–95.

Onslow, Barry, et al. May 2005. "Are You in the Zone?" *Teaching Children Mathematics.* NCTM: pp. 458–63.

Early Math Strategy, The Report of the Expert Panel on Early Math in Ontario, 2003: p. 27.

Moyer, Patricia, Johanna Bolyard, and Mark Spikell. Feb. 2003. "What Are Virtual Manipulatives?" *Teaching Children Mathematics.* NCTM.

Chapter 6

Stenmark and Bush, 2001: p. 62.

Stiggins, Rick. *An Introduction to Student-Involved Assessment For Learning:* p. 1.

A Guide to Effective Instruction in Mathematics, Kindergarten to Grade 3, 2003: p. 53.

Garthwait, Abigail, and Jim Verrill. May 2003. "Documenting Student Progress." *Science & Children.*

Wiggins, Grant P., and Jay McTighe. *Understanding by Design.* Center for Technology & School Change, Teachers College, Columbia University.

Chapter 7

Ross, Sharon. March 2002. "Place Value: Problem Solving and Written Assessment." *Teaching Children Mathematics.* NCTM: pp.419–23.

Garlikov, Richard. 2008. "The Concept and Teaching of Place-Value." The Math Forum @ Drexel University. http://www.Garlikov.com/PlaceValue.html.

The Ontario Curriculum: Mathematics, 2005: p. 25.

Kamii, Constance. 1984. *Number in Preschool and Kindergarten.*

Teaching Children Mathematics. March 2002. NCTM: p. 423.

Sztajn, Paola. Dec. 2002. "Celebrating 100 with Number Sense." *Teaching Children Mathematics.* NCTM: p. 212.

Anderson, Ann. July 1997. "Families and Mathematics: A Study of Parent-Child Interactions." *Journal for Research in Mathematical Education.* 28: pp. 484–511.

Ashbrook, Peggy. "Learning Measurement." *Science & Children:* p. 1.

Zerbisias, Antonia. *The Toronto Star,* Wednesday, July 30, 2008.

Moses, Barbara, ed. 2000. *Algebraic Thinking, Grades K–12: Readings from NCTM's School-Based Journals and Other Publications.* NCTM: pp. 5–6.

Teaching Children Mathematics. NCTM: p. 41.

Guillaume, Andrea, and Lisa Kirtman. Feb. 2005. "Learning Lessons About Lessons: Memories of Mathematics Instruction." *Teaching Children Mathematics.* NCTM: pp. 305–09.

Usiskin, Zalman. Feb. 1997. "Doing Algebra in Grades K–4." *Teaching Children Mathematics.*

Soares, June, et al. 2006. "Thinking Algebraically Across the Elementary School Curriculum." *Teaching Children Mathematics.* NCTM: pp. 228–35.

Blanton, Maria, and James Kaput. 2003. "Developing Elementary Teachers' Algebra Eyes and Ears." *Teaching Children Mathematics.*

Metz, Kathleen E. 1997. *The Assessment Challenge in Statistics Education.*

Principles and Standards for School Mathematics. NCTM, 1998.

Moscovitch, Ivan. 2000. *Probability Games and Other Activities.*

A Final Note

The Ontario Curriculum: K–8.

Appendix C   Reproducible Graphic Organizers

Text Set Organizer

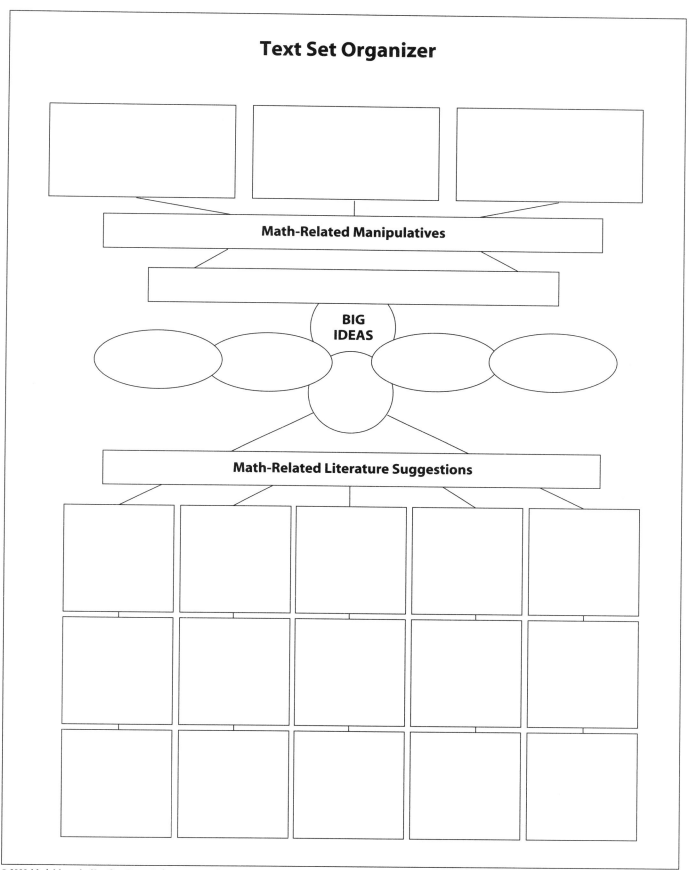

Math-Related Manipulatives

BIG IDEAS

Math-Related Literature Suggestions

Math Discovery Hub

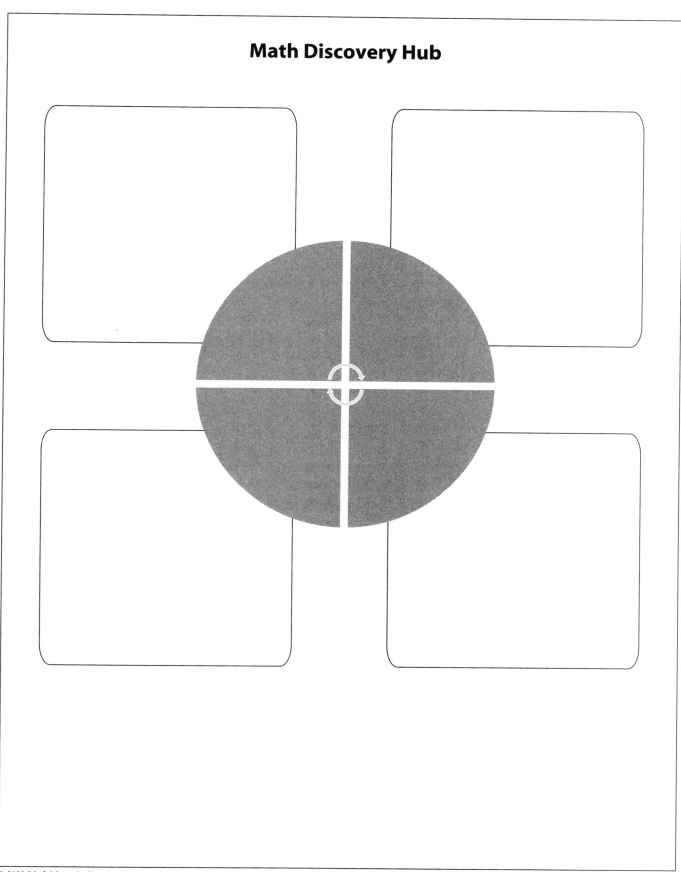

Linking Math Centre Activities and Assessment Strategies

Activity	Observation	Interview/ Conference	Portfolio	Self/Peer	Performance	Math Journal	Rubric	Checklist
1								
2								
3								
4								

Literature/Math Manipulative Organizer

MATHEMATICAL PROCESSES

Key: 1. Problem Solving, 2. Reasoning and Proving, 3. Reflecting, 4. Selecting Tools and Computational Strategies, 5. Connecting, 6. Representing, 7. Communicating

Author/Title/Type	Concepts/Skills Additional Comments	Literary Style/Type	Math Manipulatives/ Found Materials

Index